Maryland Bards
2023

Edited by
James P. Wagner (Ishwa)

Maryland Bards Poetry Review 2023

Copyright © 2023 by Local Gems Press

www.localgemspoetrypress.com

Table of Contents

AEH

It's in the corner
Of the room I'm in, stalking,
And waiting for my walls to break down
Wearing a frown
It knows I see it
Crouched on all fours, breath panting,
I reach to touch it and it snarls at me
I know better than to flee
But with the offer of
A hand, it bows its crown low,
Allowing me to pat its horned head
And it crawls up on my bed
I cradle the horned beast
Listening to it purring
It merely wanted to me to notice
It needs attention

AEH passionately writes about their life experiences and emotional struggles. Their collections encompass love letters and odes, as well as healing poetry about religious trauma and narcissistic abuse.
Follow AEH on Instagram: @juniperfae_etsy or FB @juniperandfae

Shamim Ara Akter

Me and My Conscience

Night is turning to the down
there's none,
me and my companion ,
my conscience
sit facing each other,
all the irksome things aside,
All the annoying dialogues are unheard now;
clock ticks on .
my company raised a list of objections to me
complaints going on and on
the powerbank inside the case is full ,
its heavy and the temperature is going up,
it's loaded plus .
The self's been disillusioned .
suddenly a dumb soul howls,
as if eager to explain a bad dream dreamt
urging aloud ,inside as if to a baseless well
A realization comes to the self ,
all the chaos , hustles and bustles of the day
are better than my companion.
release is needed.

Shamim Ara Akter was born in Dilpur, Feni district of Bangladesh . She was graduated in English Language and Literature, from Noakhali Science and Technology University, Bangladesh in 2019 . Her mother language is Bengali .She prefers writing in English.

Melanye Ann

The 4th Seal

Don't live your life politically, correct
me if I'm wrong.
Who's making up these rules?
Don't suffer the blind eye baiting mules,
fools…rush in
Meaningless incomprehensible jargon they feed,
come down from the steed,
that pales at the thought of its load.
The ashen and dusty road will lead you
to your rightful abode.

J. Joy "Sistah Joy" Matthews Alford

Reflections

We must look back
Vision, you see, is premised
Predicated upon the universe
In which it is formed

To see tomorrow's vision, to dream
Eyes must have a frame of reference
A vantage point through which we assess what is

But not only eyes -- minds and hearts
Indeed souls can be lifted by vision
And cursed by lack of it

So we look back
Name and claim our mournings
As freely as we seek the glory and glee of victories
Not to dwell in yesterday
Nor she in us
But to gain from her legacy, good or bad

Ancestors, elders, and tomorrow's seed yet born
Each has or shall witness
With earthly short-sightedness
That which limits vision to all this side of The Jordan

So whether we be born strong of spirit
Or weak of flesh
We are the same
And since neither war nor any of the "isms"
Which afflict mankind prevail beyond the grave
Neither free nor slave escapes the final call

We can only look back
In prayer and faith that tomorrow brings rebirth
In hopes that before or after we return to earth
Some purpose is made clear
Some deed aligned with need in a way
That our fellowship lifted another
That perhaps someone rejoiced in our being
That at least one was helped or healed by our walk

We look back
With herald or hurt, and are proud
Because we endured, we overcame
For looking back discloses
Through time's final looking glass of revelation
Our true tomorrow

J. Joy *"Sistah Joy"* Matthews Alford is the Inaugural Poet Laureate of Prince George's County, Maryland, and has authored three poetry collections. She has hosted and produced the nationally recognized poetry cable television program, *Sojourn with Words*, since its inception in 2005, and has served as president of the Poetry Ministry of Ebenezer A.M.E. Church in Fort Washington, Maryland since 2003. Sistah Joy is the founder of Collective Voices, an ensemble of native Washington, DC poets known for their social consciousness, empowerment, and spirituality poems.

Alan Barysh

Sometimes

Part A

Sometimes it is just a challenge just to un-ass my bed Depression got the best of me Sometimes my anthem is w get up? Then I remember I have work to do Tasks to finish A life to live Then I think If I successfully removed tuckass from bed sheets for a job that just barely paid the bills Then It's time to toss a blanket or two Take those meds And get on with living There's a world out there that needs changing And someone's reserved a place for me in the ranks of the world changers; can't call in sick now!

 6 Sometimes

Part B Or Never Too Poor To Lend A Hand No you only think you can think you can't lend a hand Mind you The hand might not be money The hand might be physically devoid of anything that the naked eye can see But your hand (S) are Full If there is love in your heart There is love in your hands Of there is compassion in your heart There is compassion in your hands And believe it or not You have enough Love And Compassion To share with all of creation So what are you waiting for?

Just stop and look over in the desk drawer of your soul See those pre-paid / pre-addressed Fed Ex Packages?

Just like fill up each box with what you have on hand(s) And send it off to the addressees That might be all you need

 Before Putting Notion Into Motion.

Alan Barysh is a local poet/activist who has been involved in fund and consciousness raising for the plight of the homeless and the shelters that serve them, In the past he has conducted for the composer John Cage and was poet inn residence for the tear 2000 at Maryland Institute college of Art in Baltimore Maryland.

Thais Bennett

Unspoken

Entering
this holy sin,
this is where the nightmares began...
a gift that drop from Heaven
this is where it left us-
Like this vine
dangling somewhere between space
and the sublime-
like a clock that
can actually turn back time
this
is why I'm blaming you for all these
deadly crimes
reconsidering
if you were every
a friend of mine

So why should I feel
so afraid
of needles piercing veins
marks making hearts
eyes tearing pain....
tracks from trains on veins
making it harder to explain things that once came so plain to me

I once hear you singing
"Kick it, quit it, kick it, quit it, kick it, quit it, kick it, forget it."

I once heard you praying
for things go back to the ways they used to be

But

you can't see....
I'll go crazy if I tried
I'll possibly die
I did it once before
to keep you by

I have a broken heart is what it cost
and for all it's worth
I rather feeling the hurt
of seeing you walk away
then to go another day
without these deadly games we play

You can't get by on my beautiful lies
knowing without it
our love won't survive

You can't get by on the hope
I'll take it slow

and use no more

You should know

I do love you so

this it why I can't let you go

You can't leave me to pursue your dreams
while I'm left here all alone
dealing with the demon
you have put inside
me
You are asking
"Why you don't try
to try
harder!"

if you're done
I would love to reply:

I've been hearing things
seeing things
Things
I've seen you do
and things
that were
new

things I thought
that turned out to be the true.

I keep
fighting a fight I'll surely lose
All alone

sitting here...burning needles til they bleed on it own
All because
I refused the terms
you have place upon me

I see how this is ending
with me holding on to a love
that
was doom from the beginning

I'm holding on..to no response
So
go ahead
find
your god
and get reborn.

Thais is a published poet. Her poetry have been appeared in numerous anthology including "New Breezes" by Alma Robert's". She is now a resident of Baltimore, City. She attended college in Pittsburgh, Pa. Scranton, Pa and Baltimore, Md.

Sylvia Beverly

Sometimes I Like The Rain

Pitter patter ...Pitter patter
Rain drops fall on my window sill
Massages elders aches and pains
Depletes worry of annoying ills.
SOMETIMES I LIKE THE RAIN

Gianni and Jahadah woke to find
 To their dismay, they must stay
 inside and play today
At very least we'll read good books
Accept challenge to parlor games
 will be their way.
SOMETIMES I LIKE THE RAIN.

Couples walking under one umbrella
 So in love..holding hands
Whispering about their future
 Happy to share future plans.
SOMETIMES I LIKE THE RAIN.

Forecast called for snow last
 Night
Not enough cold in precipitation's
 Might
SOMETIMES I LIKE THE RAIN.

14

Nature's soil...undying thirst smiles
 With gratitude
Soon we will witness fragrant
 varied colored flowers everywhere
 Bringing gladness to many moods.
SOMETIMES I LIKE THE RAIN.

Lovers curled comfy cozy by fire
 places
Warmth of ambers glow shines on
 Smiling faces
A beautiful night to stay home
 Listen to music a sip of champagne,
 receive God's Graces.
SOMETIMES I LIKE THE RAIN.

Sylvia Dianne Beverly, a.k.a Ladi Di is an Internationally acclaimed poet, presenting in Brixton, London, England at the Lewisham Theater. She is author of two books, "Forever In Your Eyes", Poems and "Cooking Up South", Recipes and Poems. Ladi Di has two volumes of work at Gelham Library, George Washington University.

Ava Bird

night light
lights up
the altar
shapes of animals
rocks
crystals
clocks
time
to wake up

Ava Bird is a multi-dimensional artist with a diverse collection of poetry published all over the world. Her works are printed in historical anthologies, academic journals, spiritual publications, online, recorded for radio and with music and exhibited in galleries. She is a featured guest on The New American Dream radio show on Revolution Radio for the past 12 years. Her latest book "Magical Moments" is now available.

Robert R. Bowie, Jr.

The Facts of Life

I swam, back then, with some fathers' daughters,
Backstroking only slightly out of touch,
Out to the raft in the starry waters
And never thought of their fathers all that much.

My child, don't judge me till you're fifty-five
But there were midnight visits to Ice House Pond,
In my misspent youth, when I was still alive,
Where couples would strip, and swim and then bond.

And my child, this I know for sure is true:
At seventeen we all are born to be free
But 'cause I'm your father and I love you
Please consider this seasoned advice from me:

As you lust for life avoid the crudity
But don't miss occasional sponti-nudity.

Maryland Playwright and Poet, Robert R. Bowie, Jr. has had eleven plays performed in Baltimore's Little Theaters, ONAJE, a play, performed in the New York Fringe Festival and The Grace of God & The Man Machine, was scheduled to be performed off Broadway at Theater Row in November and December, 2022 but was cancelled due to COVID. He also has a book of poems, "An Accidental Diary," which is for sale on Amazon.

https://www.robertbowiejr.com

18

Maggie D Brace

Liturgy of a New Moon

Crossing the sky with the sun by day,
shadow side pointed Earthward,
honor to the nascent moon begins.
Lunar rituals commence.

Candles set to flame, shimmer in the wind.
Elemental water baptizes anew.
Shrouded in our oaken grove,
we bathe in the sacred presence.

Setting forth our requested intentions,
we prance in the nonexistent illumination
Sun and moon in celestial conjunction,
starting our cycle of life anew.

Maggie D Brace, a life-long denizen of Maryland, teacher, gardener, basketball player and author attended St. Mary's College, where she met her soulmate, and Loyola University, Maryland. She has written *'Tis Himself: The Tale of Finn MacCool* and *Grammy's Glasses*, and has multiple short works and poems in various anthologies. She remains a humble scrivener and avid reader.

Mark Brine

Old Ones

God bless the Old Ones
Who live all alone
Exiled sadly.. their
Loved one, now gone

No one to talk to
Or share what they do
Look at the future
They'll someday be you

It bothers them so
To burden the young
Or be interfering
With youth 'n its fun

But, suffer so quiet
And wish for the past
'n wonder, how could it
Have all gone so fast

Yes, God bless the Old One
Who stares at the field
'n waits for the loved one
It never will yield

Mark Brine is a Folk-Country-Blues Singer-Songwriter, Musician, Published Author/Illustrator (Adult-Level & Children's Books) & Poet. Originally from Cambridge, Mass (by way of Nashville, Tenn.), he has lived in Maryland for many years & presently resides in the rural town of Baldwin. For more info, see www.markbrine.com

Stephen Brock

Toast

Burnt toast
Tastes of childhood
Where daily bread was in short supply,
Where "You git what you git,
And you don't throw a fit."

Realizing
With another bite
That my slab of butter
Cannot mask
The familiar taste.

Realizing
With yet another bite
That while the beast
Remains dormant
Inside me,
I can now
Choose
To discard
This black shard.

Untying the loaf again,
Selecting another piece,
Inserting it into the rectangle

Dialing down the device,
Depressing its spring,
I thank God
I need not stuff my maw
With more burnt toast.

Stephen Brock, Ph.D., teaches AP Literature & Composition and creative writing at the Montgomery Virtual Academy (Montgomery County Public Schools). Before living in Rockville, MD, he taught English in Abu Dhabi and Saigon at international schools. In his free time, Brock enjoys walking on the C & O Canal and watching film.

Michelle Burgess-Morris

You are everywhere. Yet you are nowhere to be found.
Ceaselessly I am scanning, hunting, investigating, searching for some connection.
I see you everywhere.
Why can't I find you?

Your voice is just around every corner. Your laugh calls to me.
The gray of your eyes floats in currents of the ocean.
It reflects in the sun's rays as they reflect through the clouds.
Your arm, comforting and warm, gentle and familiar, lays upon my shoulders like a blanket.
The scraggly, worn edges of your favorite ball cap seem to quickly bound through the door just in front of me.
When I reach for you, you are already gone.

It is implausible to my mind. I see you everywhere yet you are nowhere.
There is no balance, no harmony, no sense of comfort.
Promises heard as a young girl haunt me now; 5 decades into this life.
The idea that your promises were lies is simply incongruous.
You have to be somewhere!
You are everywhere.
You are nowhere to be found.

Michelle Burgess-Morris spent her childhood between the mountains of Appalachia and the oceans of the Eastern Shore. After earning multiple degrees in education, she honorably dedicated 30 years to teaching as both an elementary teacher and a college professor. Ms. Burgess-Morris has previously published two college textbooks and has research chapters featured in multiple other textbooks. A proud mother of three, she is now embarking on her childhood dream of becoming a published poet and novelist.

Wolfgang Cajina-Ledezma

A Wish

The days do feel a little shorter nowadays and with each passing moment, my body can savor the smell of your presence and the goodness it creates in my thought's feelings and my hands perceive you more and my eyes caress the pumping of both our souls' hearts, knowing each and each-other's own. What do I say? To wait for a day that's not today is not the way to play, so today I see you and with my thoughts I smell the touch of your love in my life and every day I care a little more and my being becomes less of me and more of us in both our essences' union. Today, I love you as I do my first impression and even more than the last time, I saw your eyes. The last time I saw you, it was a different world, and the birds sang and swirled, and I could see the wind twist and coil and meet the tip and top of the thoughts that were there, like an ax mob or an inside job. I wished on a star and the last time I saw you; it was a different world.

The last time I felt you, the ground hugged my skin, and the clouds carried my scent for miles and back and every hair, bristling with the shivers of your touch, murmured flirty poems as a gentle breeze caressed my earlobes.

The last time you and I were one, we walked long hours in the pastures of my mind and saw the moon in the reflection of a smile and your hands told complicated stories from the pages in demand. If I see you again, what a beautiful world.

Imagine this moment when you close your eyes; when the light has escaped, but for a second the waning of its form and look at the world in the stillness of your creation and admire its presence and embody this moment, but for a second close your eyes and imagine.

For where and when your dreams come true; wish on a star to bring back the sanity that was taken while you dreamt so hard and you wished that you were more rational than your dreams were. Wish that one day, as your eyes see the distance of your mind's dreams, you can reach the place that is more than a word in your ears when you hear the applause again and your mouth dries like it did once and the light enters your insides and your pupils dilate with excitement while you serenade the world with your soul and your body moves in ways it never did, to run its way like a river in the tide of Titans that this world has brought upon us and pour yourself with the syntony of the cacophony of the universe. For where and when your dreams come true; wish on a star!

Wolfgang Cajina-Ledezma is a poet from Silver Spring, Maryland. Author of Las Cuatro Estaciones del Lobo or The Four Seasons of the Wolf, En Pariso / In Parisus, a series of poems to commemorate some of the poems written throughout his life, Shared Lies and The Walk, two small stories. A Mortgage Professional by day, a poet by night. Wolfgang Cajina Ledezma, also attended the Music Conservatory in Managua, Nicaragua and was part of the National Orchestra at the age of 17. Now, when he is not writing, painting or making music for his videos, Wolfgang enjoys reading a good mystery, playing a thrilling board game or reading a good fantasy book.

Karissa Carson

Free

Free your voice, even when it falls upon deaf ears.
Free your voice, when you feel that no one cares.
Free your voice, let go of all the fear.
Free your voice, believe that you belong there.
Free your voice, remind them that you're not going anywhere.
Free your voice, when they give you wrong stares.
Free your voice, when faced with adversity.
Free your voice, when there's a lack of diversity.
Free your voice, even when everyone else choose to be silent.
Free your voice, sometimes the only way to avoid the violence.
Free your voice, when your voice is shaking.
Free your voice, even when your heart is braking.
Free your voice, allow your soul to awaken.
Free your voice, your silence is not up for the taking.
Free your voice, even if you're going to be misunderstood.
Free your voice, if you don't you would wish that you could.
Free your voice, for those who paved the way for our freedom.
Free your voice, because we still have a long way to go.
Free your voice, so that the next generation will do so.
Free your voice because you don't have much of a choice

Karissa Carson is the founder of Free Your Voice, a writer and motivational speaker. Free your voice is an organization that is dedicated to helping women find their voices, by offering empowerment brunches, workshops and mentorship programs.Karissa Carson is a Coppin State alumni , who majored in business management. It is her personal goal to bring hope, inspiration and empowerment to all that crosses her path. Since starting her empowerment journey Karissa has hosted multiple brunches, conducted informative workshops for PNC bank and has been featured in the Baltimore twice! Karissa is now embarking on her new journey as a self help author. When it comes to motivating others, she is like no other!

Sharon Clarkson

Mom, Friend, Confidant To The End

Ever wonder why
I don't call you Mom
Like I should
Like I could
But I would

But you are more
Then, a Mom to me
You see
Moms are like flowers
Amongst the lilies in the garden

But You, Mom,
Have class, and sophistication
That is so real
This is how I feel

Sharon Clarkson is an author, writer, poet, and professor from the College of Southern Maryland. She pursued her love of writing, releasing her first book of poetry, My Dream Book of Poetry. She released her second book of inspirational poetry, My Dream Continues, Romantic Poetry, and Prose for the Soul. Readers quickly discovered the passion in her words and the inspirational messages in each poem. Ms. Clarkson has been a guest author and performed at venues throughout the local area.

Jessica Clingman

Childhood

A broken doll stroller
A swing set without a slide
A wagon with a wobbly wheel
A shelf full of dog-eared books.

Is this a good childhood or one that leaves you heartbroken?

Two scraped knees
Two band-aids
But, no hug and kiss to make it all better.

A father who leaves
A mother who is distant
How will this little girl ever know unconditional love?

Who would think a high school math teacher would like to write poetry? Jessica Clingman does! She teaches math by day and can usually be seen after-school at one of her sons' activities with a journal in hand. Jessica lives with her husband, three teenage sons, four crazy dogs and four even crazier ducks in southern Maryland.

Michael Collins

Cecil County Sweeties

** With all respect and acknowledgement
   to Langston Hughes*

Have you dug the spill
From Fair Hill?
Cast you gims
On this pale pale thrill:

Sugar white lassie,
Blond haired treat,
Meringue baby
Sweetness on two feet.

Snug tee shirts
Tight short skirts
Atop cowboy boots
She was born to flirt

Sharp and sassy
Like wash on the line
County farm girl
Is just so fine

Daisy Dukes
And a dog named Plut'
Short and tall
Something for all

Promised her daddy
she wouldn't be late
Now she's sipping brews
on a Dodge tailgate

She's listening to Bruce
wearing old scuffed boots
Potential lovers lined
up like recruits

Michael is a playwright, with plays produced in numerous regional theaters; an actor, having appeared in over thirty productions in both community and professional theaters; and a poet, having been a contributing member of Second Saturday Poets in Wilmington, De for many years, and published in The Maryland Bards *Poetry Review*. Responding to the pandemic, Michael has written and directed over half-a-dozen Zoom-based web productions for *Socially Distant Theater*, a production of Cecil.tv. Michael is one of the founding members of *Improv on Rye, The FUNatics,* and *The Forgetful Squirrels*, sketch and improvisational comedy troupes based in Cecil County in his theater space, The Funny Farm Theater. Others have a boat on the lake or trains in the basement, Michael has a theater in his barn.

Sharon Dooley

Winter Reflections

This year winter is here with a vengeance
Temps have been below freezing for days.
As I walk with my dog
The air is frosty, clear, and crisp.
Perhaps there is a hint of snow?
The trees in the forest are stark and bare.
The deer find no shelter there.
Broken branches from a recent storm
Litter the ground.
The creek still flows, tho sluggishly
Even as ice hugs its banks.
The dog stops to sniff,
Maybe a squirrel passed this way
To find his acorn stash?
The gruff nature of winter seems to say
Abandon hope if you wander here!
But I know as night follows day
That Spring shall appear.
Soon we will see the fragile greens of spring
Sprinkled across the branches, now bare.
The cardinal pair sitting in the pine
The doves nesting under the spruce
Reinforce the hopes of life
As seed cones under the trees,
Continue that promise.

But tonight I shall be content to be inside
To sit by the fire
And continue to muse,
Or maybe to read or even write verse,
As I cuddle up with my pup on a cold winter's night.

Sharon Kay Dooley is currently a resident of Frederick MD and has lived in the state for more than fifty years. She is a semi-retired Registered Nurse and grandmother who has been writing since her teens.

John Dougherty

The Visitation

For us, Then
Had become Now (at last) –
We saw each other: A reunion.
For the passers-by in the Metro station
A Here
Would soon become (at least) a There –
A simple journey's fare
Would soon disperse this waiting crowd.
You can see
The different ways and different goals of travel –
All of us wayfarers.

And then you joined them
And left me watching –
I soon felt waylaid
By that window in the train car,
The barrier that let me
See you ride away and vanish
Yet feel a vision,
A wonderment of hope
About the surge of Space and Time,
(All mine, but just for watching and waiting),
That poured right through that pane.

John is a long time Maryland resident and was a longer time high school teacher. He tries to write at least something every day, and everyday he wishes he were still teaching.

S.J.H. Duffy

Cable TV

2A-2:30A
To Be Announced
To Be Announced
The Dark Phoenix
Comes from Westworld
On the Minight Express

The Kid
Who would be King
Gained
A Quantum of Solace
From The Nun

The Abyss
Crazy Stupid Love
Came from Bruce,
The Almighty
In a War of Worlds

Hunter-Killer
Went Off Air
In the Rundown
Fists of Fury
Were just Saturday Night Lights

To Be Announced
To Be Announced
Empire Records Dark Skies'
Side Effects

2:30A-3A
To Be Announced.....

S.J.H. Duffy (Suzuna) is a retired aerospace engineer, writer and artist; living quietly on the Eastern Shore of Maryland (Crumpton, pop.

Mel Edden

Cheese Problems

For a Brit in the States
Life can sometimes be tough,
The language, the weather,
The day-to-day stuff.

I've been here for years,
Adapting with ease,
But the thing that I miss,
Is a really good cheese.

Red Leicester and Stilton
I just love on my bread,
Monterey Jack! -
It just won't do instead!

With Branston and crackers
You'll find nothing better,
Than bright yellow butter
And a cracking good cheddar.

So, send me home for a week
And I'll visit the deli,
To buy all the cheeses
That England can sell me!

Mel Edden is a British stay-at-home mom who has lived in Maryland since 2005. She writes a poem a day and takes her inspiration from her children, nature, everyday life and her experiences of living in the USA. instagram.com/meledden

Ashleigh Elmer

The Sun

I saw the sun, then I thought of you.
Looked for the sky, but couldn't find the blue.

The sun will rise and set no matter what happens.
It is punctual, regardless of present passion.
How does the fallen rise with persistence?
Why couldn't we likewise be consistent?

How did we turn making love into a prison?
Our bended lights are locked up in a prism.
The sun shines upon us, but it reflects back.
It interrupts time like a flashback.

The sun is dazzling...My envy has grown.
As our love dwindles, it steadily *grows*.
I guess life really ain't fair, unless you're celestial.
I thought that we were on that ascended level.

We grew up in different worlds, but under the same star.
The same influence that gave purpose to our scars.
The sun has taught us that we can be ourselves no matter what.
If it can rise… then fall… then rise again… then *we must*.

I saw the sun, then I thought of you.
Looked for the sky, but couldn't find the blue.

Ashleigh Elmer, also known as Colorful Chakras in the music world, has been writing music and poetry since she was in middle school. She frequents the open mic space throughout the DMV area and has been publicly recognized for her poetry and music since 2020. Through her work, Ashleigh strives to be better than her best and she encourages others with similar experiences to do the same thing!

Mary Erikson

Ode To My Tree

I've strolled and run by you over the years
Sometimes, I glanced up and smiled at you
Other times, I paused to gaze at your beauty
Through pregnancies, trials, joys, and tears
You weathered rain, snow, wind, and dew.
Shelter from the storm, shade in the winter,
and home to countless critters was your duty
I know that nothing lasts forever in this world
You, my friend, had been around for centuries
In autumn, your colorful leaves fell in a hurtle
In wintertime, your grandeur was more visible
Come spring, sparrows sung on your branches
And in Summer your leaves glistened in the sun.
Thank you for the smiles you brought to us
A glimpse of the awesomeness of Our Creator
Maybe a new tree will take your place, it must!
A tree, like you, there was none the greater!

She is a wife and mother of three
An avid runner who enjoys the sea
A homeschool teacher, oh, Geometry
She hopes you'll enjoy her poetry
After all, she is now fifty

Elroi Eskndir

sense of space
sense of direction
is a reflection of how lost i feel
not entirely real
living a life in delusion
i'm in confusion

i'm just like not fine
feel like i'm wasting time when i'm not doing what i love
doing what you love today is tough
they sacrifice what they want to do for money
i just think it's funny
because at the end of the day

you're broke and you pray
it's gonna take a lifetime you to figure out
a life of doubt and a mind of a fool
the answer was right in front of you

Elroi Eskndir was born and raised in Silver Spring Maryland. Her dream was always to write poems and songs and one day make a career out of this. She also likes to sing, and read poetry books

Walter Jackson Fisher III

Poetic Timeless Devilish Universe

before "In The Beginning" was poetry
The universe is still "nothing" as we see
space has no form. Its not as black as can be
in that black hole sphere is inner density
we find numbers spawning illusions of we
surface projections-Devils coming from me

Walt has spent nearly his entire life on various parts of the Delmarva Peninsula. He has always been interested in the history of all forms of art. In particular, he has been captivated by the surrealist movement. He enjoys composing poems, paintings, and drawings. He has varied influences which range from Jim Morrison to Aleister Crowley. He published a book of poems called "Jewels" in 1990 and has been featured in several anthologies including Poet's Domain and Sparrowgrass.

Corey Frey

Cairn

Irish gorse's unrequited yellow
having not crept but not held back
navigated us
our tensioned expectation our
new trust tempted and given drought
missing hares
the genius loci's superstition impending
the cairn and darkness near
we turn back and carry the weight of
the unknown home

Corey Frey is a poet and visual artist living in Middletown Maryland. He has exhibited artwork throughout the east coast, which often included poetry and poetic elements and has read his work at numerous creative events. He and his wife are the founders of The Well Collaborative, a community of friends and artists dedicated to wonder, hospitality and creativity.

Rosalivet Gaines

Be Present

Show up!

See me;
Be free with me (uninhibited).

Hear me;
Steer me.

Laugh with me;
Be comfortable to gaffe with me.

Believe in me;
Conceive and Achieve with me.

Grieve with me;
Relieve with me.

Go to Church with me;
Search His Word with me.

Don't judge me;
Don't shrug me.

Be real;
Share your ideas.

Receive me;
Cleave to me.

Don't leave me behind;
Don't forget to be kind.

Please take off the gloves;
I need to feel Loved

Be Present!

Rosalivet is an aspiring poet, who only recently realized her divine gift to write poems in 2022. Her writings are an expression of life experiences, current events, and human interaction. Her goal is to write words of inspiration and truth; with hopes to bring insight to the reader and make them feel something thought provoking.

Charles O. Gauthier

The Sandpiper

A person stands
with their hands
in their pockets
looking at the pounding surf
standing at the edge
of one world
staring at another
feeling the wholeness of both.

Waves crash and claw
at the sand
their feet get wet
in the eddies
of swirling white foam
as they stand
and listens
to themself.

Having retired after 35 years of public school teaching, I finally have the time to pursue what has always been my main goal throughout my life – developing and expressing the wondrous joy of living, being fortunate to have love to share and hopefully being able to impact others with these feelings.

51

Jerry Gentry

years of mouthless gibberish
built walls around
the blues -
all the lost horizons
melt away
and then there is
craving -
a timeless want
galactic in proportion
oh those wild and random
words
and still
those laying next to me
blues,
what does the rainbow say
when caught with the mule?
the hardest pill
to swallow.
is the one that
cooks your breakfast,
Bird is gone
and Bix'
Silent echoes of the lost dawn
What does it take ?
What does it give ?
Where does the grey shaded background
end?

He started writing and submitting to the Yale Series for Younger Poets many years ago and continued to write as the rejection slips piled up. The influences to his writing style are the beat poets as well as Charles Bukowski and Richard Brautigan.

Gabby Gilliam

My Body's Memory

There is fallow earth
where my roots should be
bare toes clenching scorched soil.

My knees creak like the strained
hassock hinges that bore the weight
of my whispered prayers.

My hips curve like the snow-covered
hills they carried me over, like the crown
of the head that passed between them.

My shoulders stiffen beneath failures I fail to shed
the phantom hand that no longer reaches for them
the childhood home they can't outgrow.

Gabby Gilliam lives in the DC metro area with her husband and son.
Her poetry has most recently appeared in *One Art, Tofu Ink, The Ekphrastic Review, Pure Slush, Deep Overstock, Vermillion, MacQueen's Quinterly,* and *Equinox.* You can find her online at gabbygilliam.squarespace.com or on Facebook at www.facebook.com/GabbyGilliamAuthor.

Sara Given

To Catch a Train of Thought

Cloudburst within the mind
a torrent of rain flowing
down
shifting at every bend
every corner of the mind

a jigsaw puzzle bookcase with the secret door
just pull the right book off the shelf to reveal
a hole
new

to add to the collection
what a feat!
to get it all down before the shift
and it vanishes
over a cliff
waterfall
with the blowback of mist

enough to sense what it is
without the whole experience
of going swimming

Sara Given is passionate poet and educator. She calls Annapolis, Maryland home. The relationship between body, mind, grief and loss are human experiences that are her muses.

Michael Haldas

The Strange Gift

It's a special gift she told me.
Make sure you treat it with great care.
Endure it with love patiently.
Most people will not understand.
You'll feel like you're going nowhere,
like you're cycling endlessly;
living between hope and despair;
but holding a soul in your hand.

I hung up the phone angrily,
and I walked to the other room.
Her words echoed repeatedly.
How could anyone understand?
A gift! This was more like doom.
It bordered on insanity.
I paced and then started to fume,
yet I had to meet this demand.

Gifts were for Christmas Day morning,
birthdays and special occasions.
From the one you are adoring,
presents that make hearts feel light;
not this type of an invasion;
that made you feel more like mourning.
Despite her heartfelt persuasion,

this gift just couldn't be all right.

I walked outside in frustration,
wanting to forget her strange words.
Fuming in deep consternation,
when a gentle breeze suddenly blew.
A recollection long deferred,
carrying deep revelation;
recalling memory interred,
with sudden clarity I knew.

The memory of my father,
whose death was a sudden surprise.
Shock made me inwardly holler.
We spoke only hours ago,
but soon after came his demise.
Leaving the world without bother,
left us without saying goodbyes.
Causing deep grief that would follow.

One unusually hot spring day,
We finally cleaned the house out.
Exhausted in every way,
a cold wind blew in from the outside.
It erased my pain and my doubt.
Without words I became okay.
I knew what the Wind was about.
My grief now began to subside.

The Spirit was gracing that breeze.
It so refreshed my burdened soul.

Beyond just a strong sense of ease,
it transformed my great suffering
The wounds in my heart became whole.
Grateful I prayed thanks from my knees.
And for months I would extol,
the truth I was discovering.

But from my mind truth gets driven,
because I too often forget
The grace in life I've been given,
that I fail to appreciate.
Realization brings deep regret.
I wish I had better striven,
and not be angry when beset,
when things make my life deviate.

Now this burden was upon me,
deep suffering of another
I thought this was all behind me.
How much more pain could I take?
To avoid it were my druthers,
and I struggled internally
seek happiness said all the others.
A deeper choice I had to make.

This special gift of suffering,
yields a capacity to love
Difficult and so puzzling.
Pushes you to a painful place.
Beyond what your capable of.
The process gives a great humbling,

that can only come from above
Gifting supernatural grace.

Accepting the gift looked so strange,
to many who just didn't know
That the world likes to rearrange,
the truth to preserve its blindness.
We can deeply wish it weren't so.
Others can think we're deranged,
but the truth is it makes us grow.
Selfishness yielding to kindness.

Suffering brought out my best trait,
when I had little to offer.
Always wishing it would abate,
by grace I was illumined.
Though some played the role of scoffer,
thinking I was going to break.
Through grace I had more to proffer,
and it would make me more human.

Suffering is a cross to bear.
It's the strangest gift we receive.
It enables others to share,
from their soul's deepest reservoir.
Though we may want a reprieve.
Deep down we become so aware.
It is not something we should grieve.
We become better than we are.

Michael Haldas is an author, educator, and speaker. His published works include books (non-fiction and fiction), short stories, articles, and poems. He also has a long running podcast show and teaches online adult religious education classes.

Visit www.michaelhaldas.com to learn more about his work.

Chris Haley

Talk To Me of Long Ago

Talk to me of long ago
when dreams were everything;
they outweighed my woes.
My world lay in front of me.
I had miles to go.
Talk of when my life saw no ebbs,
only flow.
Lean into my present
from a legacy passed
long ago.
Trust you are here
because your ancestors declared,
"You, my child, are good to go!"

The author is an actor, historian, filmmaker and frequent poetry contributor to Washington DC's, Hill Rag, and the author of three poetry books: Obsessions, Until The Right One Comes Along, and the #1 rated New Release in African Poetry for April and May of 2022, Fists and Rainbows.

Tobias Stanislas Haller

The Poem to its Reader

It seems not fair to have to spend my time
imprisoned, ink on paper, on a page,
awaiting you, Dear Reader, to engage
me, read me, give life to my rhyme.
My life is spent in slumber on a shelf,
so unaware I do not know myself,
until your hand, your eye, your mind awake
me: I from you my living substance take.

But not just you, my present mortal friend,
who, unlike me, must reach a final end.
When you are dead, I'll merely fall asleep,
for I am patient, and my slumber deep.
While you are gone, another day will find
that I live still within another mind.

Tobias Stanislas Haller is Baltimore-born and raised; a graduate of
Towson State College (when it went by that name) who, bitten by
the theater bug, spent some years on the New York stage before an-
other bug — religion — bit and he entered the ordained ministry of
The Episcopal Church. Now retired (though still active) he once
more lives in Baltimore.

Lloyd Hanna

The Stem That Bears The Flower

I drank from many springs
that came from the mountains,
from seasons of rain and drought
slowly building up
with enough pressure to
squeeze through rock, purified.
Could I have known what I absorbed?
I should have heard the cold warnings
as they bubbled through the sand
and paid attention to surroundings,
because what was drunk was carried,
and mud was never fully cleared,
but if a river's path was chosen,
the way we flowed was ours,
because the destinies of waters
had their own instincts to follow.

Only reflections come from the surface,
most of what is carried lies deeper
and can't be felt until we go under
can't be known by anything
other than touch,
like the rough edge of a rock
we smooth while it scrapes us
where we thought it was a rock to stand on

when it was just another rock in the stream
like we must learn to swim
by being thrown in
and learning to tread on our own,
by hoping we can float
if we hold our breath,
but not for too long,
believing we can survive being swept up
by the waves.

I looked to the horizon for my needs,
without knowing my own feet,
or trusting the terrain,
and all the while,
if I could have stopped fighting the current
and faced my lack of self acceptance,
in the habits I internalized
to fight fear and self doubt,
to fight the fear of sinking down
I might have known:
sometimes we just have to go with the flow,
and hope that things will work out,
but changes from old flood damage don't
happen overnight,
so if the end or new beginning
is not to your liking, remember this:
water pressed and purified
by rock can bubble up through sand
without a scratch, if it is self healing.

Maybe love grows as it flows along the way,

from the waters that cleanse us,
from the things we like carrying traces of,
from the rocks we draw our strengths from,
from the saving graces living in our darkest waters,
from the things that come so close,
from the things we have to love because we have no choice,
because we must quench our own thirst to move on,
and know the love that only comes from finding our way home,
even if we don't know that it is where
we all will go, to the sea
that welcomes all waters,
saying:
Come as you are.

Lloyd Hanna has been writing since he was a teenager, and has been experiencing a recent spiritual rebirth, which is influencing his work. He performs poetry and stand-up comedy in the DMV. "He can be contacted through his instagram account, @practically _useless

Larry Hartwick

Autumn's Breath

Autumn's breath whispers
Among the conjugation of leaves.
There is no hurry.

Autumn's breath is beckoning.
There is no hurry.
The sky can wait for a while.

She gazes at the sea.
Forthcoming with the tide.
Patient is the breeze.

The blueness ripples
With subtle contours and currents.
I look upon her as she paints.

I knew her in spring.
I knew her through the endless hours.
I look upon her as she paints.

Autumn's breath is beckoning.
The maple leaf is stirring.
The beckoning beckons.

I watch as it releases its hold
With abandon and rides
The beckoning breeze.

I have watched her in spring
And in the delight of summer.
I watch her now.

She hunches over that simple table.
Paper beckoning as she stirs her palette.
Maple red swirled in ochre.

There is still the color of spring
Muted but not lost as summer
Took hold.

She traces the veins
As a surgeon would
Dark and vibrant.

I watch her now.
The palette rimming
In autumn's breath.

I watch her now
In autumn's breath.

Bernard Haske

Save These Notes

Oh darling,
please believe me:
Paul McCartney's handwritten
lyrics for *Hey Jude* just

       sold for $910,000 –
       poor Ringo, his ashtray
       only brought $35,000 –
       (see, babe, I told you –
       writing pays millions)
       so, Maria my dear,
       my northern lover – wife –
       my capital of Pennsylvania –
       my reason for daring
       border crossings and new
       citizenship –

       save these notes –

       I won't mention them in the

       pre-nup – they're all yours
       to cash in – or scatter
       them at Abbey Road –
       a reason to go back –

(maybe it won't be raining)

or post them in the Cavern
Club –they'll let you –
remind them
you got engaged there in 2019 –
where The Beatles played
292 times, many for the
Liverpool lunch crowd –
Who was playing at the Cavern
today, mate?
Did you remember my tea? –
as they were
a full-time band, no
part-time poetry –
they were serious
about
poetry:
they were young.

Maria, aren't we young?
Let's take a spin – to anywhere –
a galaxy of our own –
in that lost UFO – souped up
to 26,000 miles per hour –
with a cool racing stripe. Wherever
the Greenies are going, they'll
drop us off – I'm sure they're nice.

We'll ask them to put the top down.
The sights we'll see.

Bernard Haske is retired from The Baltimore Sun; he lives near Baltimore. His 2014 self-published collection, *The Color of Humans,* is still available on Amazon.

Monique Hayes

Planted at Lee's Flower and Card, April 1968

No blood on the birds of paradise yet,
Storefront glass a shield with Easter wreaths
Hung by my Pullman Porter that morning
Hours before Coretta's own husband fell.
Let the Soul Brother sign make them kind,
The scrawled etchings send rioters' shoes eastward.
Mama classified her Winnie as a hothouse flower,
Winding gum wrappers into garlands during funerals,
Mistaking urns for vases at white folks' homes,
But I've learned the curves of our twelve-gauge.
And though I wither at the sight of my Sonny huddled
I will cut down anyone who tries to yank him from this earth.

Monique Hayes received her MFA from the University of Maryland College Park. A Callaloo and Hurston/Wright Fellow, she recently received an American Antiquarian Society Hearst Fellowship, Ruth Stone House Poetry Scholarship, a 2022 Maryland Independent Artist Award, and an inaugural Courage to Write Grant.

Shandelle Hether-Gray

On the Corner of Blank and Blank

I, a girl of nine, could hardly know
What it was like to wear a plate glass window,
But I saw it,
Riding in my brother's car and we just kept driving.

Thrown from her car, the woman's head bounced heavily on the
ground like a soft ball
As our car slowed to get a better look,
I looked horridly at the other car
And the life it took.

The discordant sound,
Her soiled hair,
A mix of iron and twisted metal cascaded
Off her exanimate stare.

I begged my brother to call for help,
But he said, "It's already after four,
and mother expected us home an hour ago
from the grocery store."

By now, the car was impossible to track,
I looked around at the other moving cars,
And no one was looking back.
Had I imagined it, I wondered.

No one else seemed to care.
That day I realized that for most,
There is some truth in the famous line,
Out of sight out of mind.

Shandelle Hether-Gray is a licensed therapist and author, passionate about LGBTQIA representation, assertiveness, lifelong learning, and helping people find their voice.

Christine Hickey

Day's Overture

The colors in the sky above the sunset soothe the spirit
Tonight the reflected light above the clouds to the east
Painting them whiter than ever seen in daylight.
Days close so dramatically on an island.
The crescent moon drew back in the wake of the rising sun
Announced by mauve and gold.
The clouds above the dawning lifted as a glowing curtain
Advancing towards me, the cloud pulled at the brilliance,
Bringing it into view. No sound but the waves slapping
Accompanied the opening of a new day.
Trumpets before and applause following were not hard to imagine.
Walking along in the forest, each footfall pressing deep into
The pine needle mattress. The notion of sleeping on the ground
Takes on a new light.

Christine touched down in NYC,NJ,FL,NC,GA,WDC,Italy,VA and finally MD in 2018. Much travelled and long lived, making her first attempt at crossing from shadow to written word as expression of visions in later life. A painter, pollinator-wildlife gardener.

Charles Hilton

The Progress Pitch
I am Progress, a dealer in hope
Pushing techno-salvation as dope
I'm a Star Trek movie, a Jetson cartoon
A science fiction novel, a hot air balloon
Bloated with images floated across your mind
Enticing you with thoughts of a future divine
Massaging the message, tailored to your ears
Keeping you dreaming, playing on your fears
Resistance is futile, I am the page and the pen
The narrative written from beginning to end
Indulge without worry; wash, rinse and repeat
Till you think no more, a slave to the beat
I am the owner, you have been bought
I will direct you, no need for thought
Onward and upward the clarion call
A deranged chorus, deceiving you all
Forget Mother Earth, animals and sod
Who needs nature when Progress is God

Charles Hilton is a retired handyman and native of Baltimore with a bachelor's in history from Towson University. Raised by a single-mother-barmaid with four siblings, Chuck has seen and lived the wild and tragic side of life, His blog is agreenfedora.wordpress.com.

Lynn Holmes

I write; you paint.

I write; you paint.
Deal.
But first I must purchase a new one subject college-ruled spiral note-
book.
Done.
$4.99 plus tax.

I write; you paint.
But what should I write about?
My thoughts are dark and melancholic.
Express yourself, regardless. Pain.
Depression.

I write; you paint.
Will you use the $40 per tube paint?
Do it.
There's no time like the present.
The present is the only time you have.
Use your favorite brush.

I write; you paint.
Catastrophic musings swirl in my brain.
Dare I put them on paper?
Or do I let them float unrequited?
Spew them.

Do it.

I write; you paint.
Landscape.
Still life.
Portrait.
Abstract.
What or who inspires you?

I write; you paint.
Six stanzas strong.
How do I feel?
Grim. Gloomy. Glum.
Dismal. Despondent. Dispirited.
Nowhere to go but up.

I write; you paint.
Deal.

Lynn Holmes is a retired middle school English teacher who now enjoys exploring life through poetry.

Sandra Inskeep-Fox

The Artist of Marriage

The young couple asked the old woman to read <u>The Art of Marriage</u>
At the ceremony. They gave her a copy and she read.
The mind of an old woman wanders; the text was after all
More cryptic than her memories.

Which artist could paint the marriage she knew? The list
Of possibilities was long and varied. Matisse with his cut-outs
Would try to put each thing in its place. Nothing she could remember
Fit perfectly. Jackson Pollock with his noxious habit
Of slopping paint everywhere knew what some days were like.
Warhol captured the absurdity of it; Picasso, its strange twists and
cuts and misplaced
Edges of happiness. Cassatt was too flowery; O'Keefe, bland as a
shopping trip
To Walmart.

Van Gogh,
She settled on Van Gogh. She wanted to tell the gathered crowd
What she was thinking, what Van Gogh knew:

How everyday was a series of new visions to be captured on canvass;
How trudging to the center of the canvass was the first step of creating
art;
How passion could roll across the stretching fields of green
And burst suddenly into a giant sunflower, one among many;

79

How the long furrows of rich soil were ripe for treading
And all lead home again;

How stars in free fall, as they had been when she and Mr. Wonderful
Met, still fell, never settled but floated and fell in some great shower
Of abundance

And abundance settling, became a reflector of memories;
How great cushiony choirs of clouds made way for the pointed
Sturdy needs of cypress trees;

How raucous murders of crows, half hearts of laughter, rose
And swished against the night
Which became then the softness, the magical together-
Aloneness, glowing gold outside a Paris café.

She wanted to tell the couple that The Art of Marriage was only a
vague
Sketch of what marriage could be.

Sandra Inskeep-Fox has been published in Chaffin Review, Facet, Cimarron Review, Commonweal Magazine, Virginia Woolf Miscellany and others. She is currently at work on a novel about coming of age in Housing projects in the 1950s.

Jeffersonian Jeff

Oh Maryland my merry land
Bound by the North and South
In the middle, but not in between
Tolerant of every religious condition

Home of Liberty's battlefields and fortresses

To thee I sing

A little America with all there is to see:
Farms and fisheries
Cities of commerce
Seats of government
Laboratories of invention and discoveries
Trails and trials of freedom's ideals

Your bay is the estuary that
measures the health of Earth
May your ecology set us free
from all of society's toxicity

No one knows what's to be our destiny
Ever keep your heraldry a banner of honor
Yours is a symbol of harmonious diversity

To thee I sing like Francis Scott Key.

Jeffersonian Jeff is the "Purveyor of Rock n' Roll Poetry, Prose, Songs, Comedy, and Commentary on Democracy and Self-Government in the Republic of the United States of America." He writes to encourage everyone to resist hypocrisy within, and be civil, civically minded, neighborly, well informed, and politically active. He asserts that citizens in democracy must lead society with exemplary character, pressing for justice and liberty for all.

leslie Peace jubilee

Sonnet from the Lovelorn

How much do I hate you? Let me spell it out.
I hate you throughout all time and space.
I hate you for upsetting my place
In the Universe. I hate your sexy pout.
I hate you to the level of the clout
I lack, my poverty proved a severe case.
I hate you. I'm enslaved by my huge smile
Whenever you look my way. I might as well shout
Out loud, 'Oh, my God, he's the one I want!'
I hate you with all my passion you refuse—
You flirt with me just enough to taunt.
In your arms for a second before your eyes accuse
Me of desire. You let me go, I feel gaunt
And gouged out. You are my forever Muse.

---

leslie Peace jubilee was born in Baltimore, Maryland where she began writing poetry at the age of four. She has an MFA in Creative Writing from Sarah Lawrence College and was voted Baltimore's best poet for 2017 in the Best of Baltimore Readers' Poll. She is the author of two poetry chapbooks and **sing caged bird: compassion cards for journaling and contemplation**. She continues to reside in Maryland with her rabbit, Chi Kozi.

Maggie Kaprielian

How to Console Your Grieving Younger Sister

i. Get out of bed when you hear her sobs at midnight.

The walls separating your bedrooms are thinner than the list of your unshared memories. Your eyes are only half-adjusted to the darkness, and her screams are equally thunderous as they are devastating. As tempting as it is to bury your ears between the white linen sheets, realize that compromising your sleep isn't such a compromise when it comes down to the agony of your sister.

ii. Ask her what's wrong, but don't get defensive when she won't tell you why.

You and her talk incessantly. Survival seems unpromised on days where you don't communicate til you've hit the extremity of silence. But sometimes, shared silence can be just as soothing as an: are you okay? Sometimes, talking is overbearing when your own mouth mistakens explanations for screams. She doesn't owe you words, even after the fifth time asking. Remember that your presence is the fondest gift when compared to absence. So sit with her in this silence. Don't make her listen to it alone.

iii. When she finally tells you the reason for her weeping,

prioritize the clouded eyes right in front of you. When you hear his name, you'll long for nothing more than to to wreak havoc on the life who's responsible for your sister's suffering. Save the unadulterated pettiness for the morning. In this moment, all of your attention should be directed to her. Do not tell her that she's wasting her time over a boy she won't remember in five years. You've told her that before, and although it's entirely true, she doesn't need to hear it again. Let her feel the fury of Ancient Greek goddesses, stripped of their own salvation. Let the wrath Aphrodite speak volumes in your sister's bedroom.

iv. Do not leave her bedroom until she falls asleep. But when she

asks for space, go down to the kitchen and pour her a glass of water. She's not the same freckle cheeked, baby toothed sister she once was. She doesn't need her hand held but she still needs to know someone cares enough to reach out their open palm. She can make decisions, so let her make decisions. Listen. Absorb her words. Give her water but let her form a vast ocean.

v. Realize you've been here before.

You and your sister aren't too different. You've had nights parallel to these; full of looming thoughts as the world grows too quiet. You've boarded doomed ships before, unaware of the colossal storms preparing to flounder your strength. The only difference is, she has you. So see yourself in your sister. Sit with yourself from years prior:

Get out of bed for her.
Don't get defensive.
Prioritize her emotions.
Do not leave her bedroom.
Pour her a glass of water.
Share the silence that was
always too loud for her.

Maggie Kaprielian is a poet from Montgomery County, Maryland. She is currently an Editor-in-Chief for WInston Churchill High School's literary arts magazine, Erewhon. She will attend Emerson College during fall of 2023 to pursue her studies in writing, literature, and publishing.

Rishidev khatak

I Lived There Once

"Look, I used to live there,"
A place I once called home.
Full of white walls,
The doors ajar.
Kids running free,
No matter its cold or hot.

It is noisy and,
The people speak loud.
Many cars go,
up and down.

The train station is near,
The horn it blows,
No matter what time,
the day calls.

A rainbow of people,
From every part of the world.
All at this place,
I once called home.

But the place is no more,
The door left ajar.
The chit-chat has stopped,

Even the spring has gone.

Once my home ,
Now is just a general apartment.
Like a kiss in the air,
It has no emotional layer.

It has become a hollow tree trunk,
A creek with no water,
A bridge to serve no travelers,
The people are gone!
With them the life of this house.

Rishi started writing poems just a few years ago. As an aspiring An-
thropologist, he likes to write about his experience with people and
nuances he sees in the society. He is a fan of animated TV show,
Bojack Horseman.

Latoya Kidd

The grim fiancé

Something is not right about the man your going to marry
He is weird and secretive
His eyes are dark with no soul
When he visit the house for a party and I went into the garage
To get a case of soda he pushed me onto the ground and and assaulted
me
The threaten me is I told a soul
When I got up and went to the bathroom I cried
You tell me about the wedding that she is happy to have
But I my mind he is nothing but a monster
I went to the police station to make a report they told me a
About his criminal history with women
He marries then and rape them and kills them
I told him what he did to me and they found my breast
The police said to tell my sister
When I left the police station I called her up crying and I told her
What her fiancé did to Me
She she ferrous laughed and hung up the phone
At that point i she told me that we are going to Mexico to get married
I begged and pleaded with her not to go
But she hung up the phone and left for Mexico
Three days later I got a phone call and it was from the police
A woman has been raped and murdered
They need me to identify the body
I took the next flight to Mexico

To identify the body and and I cried and I saw my sister dead
She was shot three times in the chest
I warned her to not marry this man
We took the body back to Chicago and we had a funeral I cried along
Out mother who cried if her sister and daughters that we lost
To a monster

Latoya has written many different topics on different subjects. Latoya started writing for the Owl newspaper: Newspaper Article: Are you ready to have a baby? Newspaper Article: Theft is not a good behavior Newspaper Article: A degree means more Prince George's Community College. Latoya begin to submit manuscripts to Reflections literary magazine Manuscript Fiction Poem: Backdoor woman, Manuscript Fiction short story: Royalty, Manuscript Fiction short story: Waiting for my African prince to return. Latoya went on to submit more manuscripts in Off the coast magazine Manuscript Fiction poem: the pork back Barbecue Man. Latoya has submitted manuscripts for the dirt magazine Latoya has submitted manuscripts in pink panty magazine Manuscript Fiction poem Its none of your business.

Millie Landrum-Hesser

Snow Monster Procession

The bus climbed
   the mountain
   through the ring of clouds and
all the trees changing to
Pine, only pine
and then no trees
only permafrost monsters
of gnarled white,
   Inside-
   Live with tree spines.
   They stood in a ring at the very tip
   circled round and round
   in celestial stasis
   the air powder white
   clouds far below obscuring valleys
like so many reflections
   on a still clear lake

The layers of sky and earth and
water and sky
   all tied together
by molten rock
mounded
cooled
volcanoed.

In the chugging bus we
  smoked the glass
  mouths pressed
  too charged to speak
Ions melted in the air
and hair ceased swaying
humbled stasis
Charges taking place.
We could see a shift in light
as the sun processed
from figure to figure
all crystal and white
and we closed our eyes
our minds shut
  Silence
Wind
Luck

Writer/songwriter Millie Landrum-Hesser grew up in California and Maryland. Her quirky, surreal style is further influenced by several years teaching, travelling, and writing in Japan and Asia. Her work has appeared in *Seventeen*, a Coachella music sampler, and the Japanese anthology *Shira-shin*, among others. She and James Hesser record and tour as the music duo Waterplanet. She has two children, Phoebe and Ivan, and teaches writing at Towson University.

Jane Leibowitz

Being Let Go

Yesterday you walked beside me.
Not today.
Walking back to the house,
I saw your smaller footprints in the snow, outlined next to mine.
The snow would eventually melt.
Your footprints would blur,
then disappear.
And that would be the last we'd be together.
Living together.
After that there were visits. Short ones.
Always bringing more discomfort
than the anticipated joy,
the ever-optimistic mindset
leading up to The Visit.
Until the optimism waned.
Then, even the visits.

Jane Leibowitz thrives on the eastern shore of Maryland, taking inspiration from the people, the countryside and the sea. Writing, painting and cooking are the fruits of her creative labors. She is currently working on illustrating her book of original haiku.

Angelo Letizia

The things I wish I took for granted

I have some good memories
And things I am proud of
And things I worry about
But I am not certain
Any of this matters
My wife has slept with other men before me
And my son dropped a pass
People I love are sick
And still
I don't think any of this really matters
Because the room divides space into
Boxes, shapes of despair
And they live
Where god used to be

Angelo Letizia is a professor of education at a college in Baltimore. He has published four books of poetry. He lives in Manchester with his family.

Nereida Mangosing-Koeppen

Shangri-LA

1

I remember when I was a slip of a girl
Weary at the end of the day in school
not eager yet to face the chaos at home, I
walk down to the open sea.

It is a short distance from my home
A concrete wall shelter the town from the shore
Afternoons at high tide and heavy rains
Surf scales the wall, forms a beach on both sides.

I wade in the foaming briny waters
running liberated onto the beach.
I bask in the warm caress of my feet, toes
tickle, as I run barefoot on the powdery sand.

I scour this favorite haunt for myriad treasures
from which I weave fabulous plots and fanciful casts
driven by my girlish fantasies and desires
to someday read to my children from my book.

2

Our family leaves the beloved town, moves
to the city to expand the childrens' horizons
The beach at the edge of town, earns a choice

place along with my childhood toys.

The people, the poems and the tales I created
seem silly and trite, shrink to mere childhood folly
Life replete with bridges to cross and fires to put out
More urgent than momentary sparks of whimsy.

3

One day back in town to the seawall I run
to that dear spot and the little girl I think I am
Eager to revive long-lost joys to explore
Free from the weight of adult burdens and chores.

Alas the beach that spawned a thousand reveries
is gone. Cause the town has breached its seams.

I sit on the wall and grieve my lost childhood
with all the countless things I have loved and lost
Bereft but resigned I get up to depart, but
a cool breeze wafts over from the other side

dripping with the salty essence of the sea.
and a beguiling thought that brings solace to me.
The sea is water, waves, currents, and tides
It cannot breathe or dream or hope.

But I live, I love, and all my hopes and dreams
deeply entrenched within my being's core
Quiver to be touched with new fire.

Nereida Mangosing-Koeppen graduated with a BA in Literature with a major in journalism at the University of Santo Tomas in Manila, Philippines. She also took courses towards a Masters Degree in English Literature at the Ateneo de Manila University which she did not complete before she moved to Washington, DC in 1972. She completed an MBA with a major in International Business at the George Washington University. After 32 years at the World Bank, she is enjoying her retirement singing at her church choir, writing poems and her journal and traveling whenever she can.. A resident of Washington DC for 32 years, she currently resides in Silver Spring, Maryland with her husband.

Kari A. Martindale

Pedestal

Humans reduced to pranks
the elite play on the elite;
the tired and poor, they huddle
in planes and buses,
masses of singing telegrams
yearning to breathe free.
Political refuse, brazenly tost at the feet
of wretched vineyards and teeming mansions,
where lamps are turned off and golden doors locked
while America's lips remain silent.

Kari Martindale is a Pushcart Prize-nominated poet and spoken word artist who has been published in various literary journals and anthologies. She sits on the Board of Maryland Writers' Association and is co-editor of Pen-in-Hand. She has an M.A. in Linguistics, manages EC Poetry & Prose, and values kindness over niceness and justice over peace.

Paula H. Mathis

Words...The Poet's Posture

they flow so free inside of me
they rise like yeast in sweet rolls
a taste so sweet my soul does eat
to purge them as I speak
no paper no pen can quench the thirst
to spew them from inside
and give them life that spins a tale
of a journey no longer I hide
they sing a song that lingers
their rhythm has no rhyme
they are just words they tell a story
of adventures in my lifetime

Paula H. Mathis was born and raised in Washington, DC. She is wife to Larry and Mother to Eboni, Kareem, Shannon, and Lawrence. After high school she attended college where her talents in communication, specifically writing, would surface. Always consumed with writing creatively, she would eventually realize that written expression is a gift. She immersed herself in the art of writing poetry of various styles, but her heart would be anchored in writing for the Lord. She is known by many as, "God's New Testament Poet". Her style embodies that of the Biblical poets; prophetic in its muses, proclaiming "Messages from Heaven". As an Evangelist, Author, and Poet, she uses poetry and plain talk to seek those who are "Lost in the Storms…" of life, the title of her first book. She uses her poetic gifts and personal testimony as she continues to walk out her purpose, sharing "Words" as her poetry directs, strengthens and encourages those who seek change in their lives, as well as "Shelter from the Storms.." life can bring.

Dorothy Mbori

Celebration

A new day has come.
The sun has risen again.
The rays of the sun stretch out into the horizon,
Embracing us with its warmth.
A new day has come.
Swards of grass sway gracefully in the wind,
Dancing to a beautifully haunting silence.
The whisper of the wind soothes our traumatized souls.
The flowers blossoming in the gardens,
Enchanting bright petals sparkle on the horizon,
like the waters on a lake when the sun hits it just right.
We still remember the days of yesteryear,
When darkness reigned.
A gathering gloom hung over us like a heavy gray cloud.
The days of yesteryears,
When the certainty of tomorrow was unassured.
The days of yesteryears,
When smiles were scarce and laughter was muffled.
We suffered losses,
We endured emptiness,
We waited for good news,
But were bombarded with bad tidings.
The silence in our spaces was deafening,
And we craved the company of those we took for granted.
But still, we held on and didn't lose hope.

A new day has come
and with the new day,
We move forward with certainty.
We gather like the dancing queens at a carnival,
celebrating the freedom, we craved for months.
Finally, the silence is replaced by sounds of laughter,
Music blaring in the distance,
Flowers Blooming in the fields,
Bright red and yellow petals,
Blinding us with their beauty.
Finally, our faces glow with beautiful bright smiles
And finally,
We can share life, and love, and happiness
A new day has come, And finally, we can breathe.

Dorothy Mbori is a Maryland author and poet who has published two young adult fantasy adventure novels. She enjoys sharing her poetry with the Asbury Methodist Village poetry club members. Her poetry has appeared in the Asbury Campus publication, The Village Life, and has won a couple of their poetry contests. When Dorothy is not writing, she enjoys learning new things, reading, and spending time with family and friends.

William McNeil

Dear Lord Suite, #34

On hearing the summons to return home
the Spirit began preparations for ascending this world.

And as customary, Ego was ever present grasping madly
and insisting on the right for more time together.

And as sure as the sun rises to later meet the moon's beauty—
and with the momentum of sunlit clouds across a vast blue sky

did the Spirit begin to turn and gaze at its brother—
who had fallen long ago to shadow.

And with a brilliant radiance which would permeate all physical
matter
the Spirit began to manifest wave upon wave, upon

wave of light—
everlasting light.

William McNeil is an elementary school teacher with the Prince George's County Public School system. Prior to following this career path as an educator, McNeil also worked for six years in South Korea, as an English/Photography Instructor in the department of General Studies at Hanseo University. Inspired by the music of John Coltrane, and the natural world, McNeil began the 'Dear Lord Suite" as an offering to his divine source.

Laurel Mendes

Love creates change

If we truly love, we have to allow the change.

Love reshapes us so there is room within us for it to dwell,

And grow.

Soon, we find ourselves changing for it, again and again.

Making room,

This or that time, not just for love itself,

But for all those random, even wayward, hearts, it takes into it's keep-ing.

Learning from us learning from it, we are shown there is always more love, somewhere,

To nourish,
To prosper,
To cherish,

Love, for which, we will change more still, until we barely notice at all, we are changing.

The habit of changing for love, is now the rule, not the exception.

Even the exception only truly troubled and frightened us the first few steps on the journey.

Along the way, we got worn in.

We became love's comfortable old shoes.

What an extraordinary fate— holy and full of grace.

Stacey Merola

Ode to My Childhood Couch

Velvet couch
Black, red, and white stripes
I push my finger through the plush
Changing the fabric from dark to light

8-track tape player nearby
I put in Simon and Garfunkel
And bounce joyful
As Boxer's cannons erupt

My perch to witness
Elvis' death and a city's blackout
My velvet realm
It was enough

Stacey Merola, Ph.D. is an educational researcher and program evaluator who lives in Chevy Chase, MD. When not working she enjoys writing, taking her son on adventures, running, playing piano, and taking road trips to Maryland crab decks.

Pamela Michaels

Table for One

Table for one
Small island of Joy
I'll gladly rent
Your space in my time

Table for one
With a coffee and scone
Refuge from many
The frantic and loud -

Who needs the onslaught
 Of everyday talk;
I'll smile in the silence
 And bask in some thought

 Of a faraway Paradise
 Brimming with light
 Rainbowed with parrots
And amythest hills
Cerulean slices
Of tangerine song
At my table for one.

Table for one
Small island of Peace -

Maybe later I'll care
For a table for more

But here in this now
Of a singular place
I'll say my small grace
 For the table for one.

Pamela has been immersed in the various Art forms during most of
her 72 years; Music and Visual Art were prominent in family life. It
was difficult to choose a major in College, but Art won out and Pam-
ela spent much of her time teaching Art to Special Education Stu-
dents. Music, in the meantime, became a vocation, and out of that
songwriting appeared, with lyrics shifting to poems on occasion. Her
poems tend to imagery that reflects her life experiences.

Tina M. MWP

Aureum Momentum

On a Spring morning with sinking air
the sky the color of a robin's egg
the meadow in the park at the end of the street
serves an *aureum momentum*.

When the Earth's bow reveals the sun
the trunks of slender pines slice rays into lines,
tips of black fractal oak branches
scatter light in uneven crosshatches.

With arms stretched out wide, stand in the meadow
face the monstrance that appears between the trunks
turn in a circle like Earth on its axis
follow the fanned-out rays around:

the tips of the red oak buds gold more than green,
the school in the pond on the meadow's edge
orange like the anther of the purple crocus,
tee-yees of finches echo like Tibetan singing bowls.

Tina M. MWP (she/her) serves others through her professional life as an engineer and innovator in public health, and in her personal life, as a volunteer and tutor, and now, as a writer. Her first published poem, *A Time to Rest,* appeared in New Verse News. She writes creative nonfiction and poems about belonging, identity, and nature. She lives with her family in Rockville, MD. @TinaM_MWP

Scott Myers

Amethyst sunset
Draping dusk in velvet puffs
Heavens resplendent

Allergens abound
Ants dance and prance upon me
Histamine footprints

Scott Myers is a Maryland based musician, who creates ethereal ambient music, plays in a horror-punk rock band, and bass guitar for an indie-folk duo. His melodic rhythms and deep beats fuel his stoic, condensed poetic voice, which prizes quality over quantity.

Jason N

Deluge

i take all of these photographs
and hope to capture bits of you
a story told that may unfold
amongst some drops of dew

a golden glow below these leaves
this breeze to lift me a bit higher
a certain hue within this view
with a glimpse of something brighter

a yearning shore a bay that roars
these waves that crash a little closer
this glowing moon a tide that swoons
a break that's looking for some closure

i'll try to capture all of you
in little pieces of my day
a story told on sunset strolls
simple words just can't convey

Jason is a Maryland poet and photographer. Striving to capture and share the beauty of the Chesapeake Bay.

Douglas Orr

From Lonely Ivory to Orange Rage

There is nothing more,
that can be said,
Or done,
To save us, and our fellow creatures,
from ourselves, and our rendezvous with destiny.
We can only grieve, for a soon to be, lost world.

The quest for palm-oil plantations is relentless,
Beckoned onward, by cosmetics,
and processed food consumption.
The sound of heavy machinery permeates the Borneo air.
Anger, raw emotion, thrust the large primate forward.
Using long aggressive strides atop its felled tree trunk,
The orange, spindly-arm ape defiantly and determinately
approaches the blade of the big forest destroyer.
With a rapid blow to the blade it strikes and tumbles
Back down to the log-strewn debris of fallen timber.
It sullenly arises to its feet and stumbles defeatedly away.
Who cries for the Orangutan's lost habitat?
Where is the sorrow of the grief stricken,
Who oppose these invaders and pervaders
of crimes against the web of life?

The quest for fossil fuel sources is relentless.
The seismic air gun blasts from exploratory ships,
penetrate the deepest seas of the Atlantic.
A mammoth sized, 100-year old creature
glides through the blue, migrating to polar seas.
Startled, stressed, and confused by these
ambient reverberations, that obliterate the
sweet songs of distant relations.
The deeply scarred mother and calf dodge an
array of fast moving commercial factory ships.
They pass a Right Whale as it struggles to
Free itself of entangled fishing net gear.
Where are the sea captains to be found,
who cry out to protest the treacherous habitat
Navigated daily by the Baleen Whales?

The quest for minerals and rare-earth elements is relentless.
Global technology is thirsty for new raw materials,
to build an emerging green-energy platform.
The blasting, scraping, and drilling sounds
of mining operations invades the bucolic,
lush land of southwestern China.
A herd of 15 giants begins a 300-mile trek northward,
to escape a land supposedly conserved for their well-being.
Led by "Broken Trunk", and monitored by drones
circling above, they plod through orchards,
rubber plantations, tea fields and towns.
"Civilization" is awe-struck by the spectacle
of their incredible odyssey.
What restlessness motivates this extended family,
Including one newborn, forward, toward the unknown?

Fight of the great ape,
It is not.
But is it the flight of the giants?
Where is the tear shed for the Asian Elephant's lost habitat?

Following the creed of Native Americans,
We must look and listen to wildlife in a
New, Reverent, and perhaps Mystical way.
Using senses we have long lost through atrophy,
They send us an urgent warning:
"Your rapacious appetites
to consume, must be quelled."

Over eleven thousands of years,
Our Wild Planet achieved a delicate balance
For the complex web of all life forms,
Including a stable global climate for that life.
Man's dominance has upended this harmonious balance
Of the Holocene Epoch in only a few hundred years,
A mere blink of geological time.

It cannot continue.
It must not continue.
We are the stewards of the Planet and of
All God's Creatures, both Great and Small:
Tree Dwellers, Swimmers, Plodders, and Flyers.
Our Duty for their Survival and of Ourselves
is owed to the
Vast and Ancient Cosmos,
From which we arise.

The Second World War comes abruptly to an end,
And the Atomic Age begins with
The second ever nuclear blast,
used destructively by Man.
The bomb duo crushes two cities and 200,000 people.
One continent away from this radioactive fallout,
The last stand of oak trees are felled in the
swamps of the great bottomland forest.
All for elegant, sewing machine cabinetry.
And from this flattened primeval forest,
the very last Ivory Billed Woodpecker
calls out her final sad refrain for any
nearby soulmate who may be listening.
"Kent-kent" she cries.
The sound of silence is the reply.
"Kent-kent", she cries again.
No other Lord God Bird is listening,
Nor Humanity.

Douglas Orr is a retired electrical engineer who is now active as an environmentalist, historian, artistic photographer, and poet. He lives tranquilly in his home in Harford County, Maryland with his wife Cynthia, and their faithful Weimaraner and Dachshund companions. His creative work can be viewed and read at https://dworr.zenfolio.com.

Carlo Parcelli

Vesper

Thou hast undone the world
    By thy unraveling
And thy raveling but mocks the thing.
    And of this making a mad king
      What prate before thee,
For there is no longer gospel nor creed
    But be this hairy beast,
The emptied chalice of his being.
There, freedom has its sack of wind
    The spine to bullwhip the earth
Because this end will have no clue
      Of its beginning
  Not even laughter for nothing be true to it
For the cockroach even in victory don't snicker
    Or be so prideful as to bake his own crust
    And barter existence upon it.
I can point is - is – is,
    But cannot say what need be said.
 Not even cast this be
    Of vermin's wit. And so you have
Ended your catechism and with your bum
    So, piles or no, grind upon it.
      You know the word.
It biddeth time as it doth reside upon itself.
    Monkeys mock us for they

Veered toward perpetuity
As we be pickled in a godhead
And for shame bury our dead
Taunt time about a fancied resurrection
While taking our liberties to a new extinction.
Destiny be not visited on fools
But the wisest of the immolated.
Call me the Vesper.
I know not nor care what you mean
For you mean nothing to me
As made inkling of your body
Still concealed is no gadgetry to cheat eternity
But to be cheated in its glory.
What to be thy own butcher,
Such privy nature and cobbled law
That slaughter hath but your scribbling upon it.

It's been one long Fall since
That chain of indifferent acids
Dripped upon you
And you took that epiphany
As an omen for redemption.
A way to climb out of your skin,
To deny the fluke of 'too late';
That there is no prophecy
A descent preaching it has been.
Booby trapped formulas
That shuck the masks
Our weakness grows;
The core somewhere lost in the cloud
The cloud a most succinct 'I don't know'.

Where did it go between time's creasing?
    To pop up the right answer;
  Corrigible for the moment
Then dangerous and false;
    Idolized idolatry
That left its brains upon the pavement
  As a calling card for getting it wrong.
An invitation from the catechorium
    To do it again
  Ever closer to Zeno's punch line
When the endtimes make
    The morning's funny papers.

That was not me just scampered over your feet
  Or buzzed your ear and trashed your sleep.
Not me what piffles your dreams
  Or hampers your yarn.
At East Coker when we went to bed
    She bore a death's head
  Just above her birth canal.
And I watched my prick
  Glide like a slide trombone.
I had her, then I had her sister;
  I could feel the daggers
The moment I kissed her
  So I fell to my knees
    And gave her head.
A kid in our foxhole said
  You can make anything sound good
Even grief and dread.
  His corpse curdles in a shallow grave.

His overnight bag emptied to the afterlife,
   Anointed with his rolling papers
      And his after shave.
The Shit saved us all
   For after that math nothing
  Ever again rose to the level of depraved.
And I learned to write
     Like there's no tomorrow
  And you're in everybody's.
That a putz that can upend time's arrow
    With infinite sorrow?
  Who is talking denouement now.
     And how?
For the sword be not Damocles',
   Who but for a day
Lived his life upon his knees.

Carlo Parcelli has published 6 books of inchoate & highly offensive verse which fortunately have reached virtually no audience at all. His latest volume, 'Tarrare & Other poems' published by New Generation Beat Publications won 'The Devil Take the Hindmost Award' for execrable verse for the year 2060, the same year Isaac Newton predicts the world will end. Who wants pizza?!

John Patnode

She Sings Sea Songs

I took my dear sailing
O'er the sea,
Her voice like an angel
Singing to me.

She went in the water
My beautiful miss,
I heard her singing,
It sounded like this.

Gargle gargle gargle
Ga-garglety garg!

She sang me a new song
I'd not heard before,
I went to the bow sprit
So I could hear more.

She sang with a frenzy
With passion and gile,
I poured a new whiskey
To listen awhile.

Blubble blubble blubble
Blu-blubbety blub

She came to the song break
And yelled "Throw a line!"
"I wish that I could dear,
But I just can't rhyme. "

She started a floating
A flat on her back.
She spit out some water,
My baby humpback.

Spppphhhhhhttttt!!!!

Looking back now with some
Morbid reflection;
She brought her act to a
Sinking direction.

She sings her love songs
To the mermaids so deep,
But she rings me a bell
When fog starts to creep.

Dingety dingety dingety
Ding-dingety ding!

Robin Payes

Amber Eyes

February dawns wearing amber eyes
And I am a flyspeck trapped in that morning's
Honey-thickened gaze. I need to fly but my
Wings are congealed, sticky-thick.

Winter ebbs, teases with the promise of spring yet-
To-emerge. Green-helmeted buds erupt, setting out
Tentative antennae so as to one day sprout
Their joy at life. They are frozen in time.

Crocus, daffodil, narcissus: I whisper their names.
For they are as stuck as I under winter's heavy coat,
Stilled by snow-tempered passions, trembling
To thaw into a spring-sunned earth.

We dare to hope. That is the essence of the season.
Even hunched under the weight of gray gel,
Life burbles, patiently planning a return to life.
I long for a glimpse: Crocus, daffodil, narcissus!

"Be still, Robin." They whisper my name. For I too
Emerge with spring. "Be patient." The stuck-ness lasts
An unearthly moment. Sun will soon soften the honey-glazed
Sunrise, uncongeal the quickening spring.

Robin Stevens Payes is a Rockville, Maryland-based writer. She is author of the Edge of Yesterday teen time-travel adventure series, and creator of the online, experiential "learning through story" portal at edgeofyesterday.com. She leads writing and creativity work-shops for teens, and will be launching, The Mother-Daughter Code, a six-week coaching program giving busy moms of teenage girls breathing room, in 2023.

Louis Petrich

Love Lesson #2

I don't.
 Hold it against you? No.
How could I?--
          grateful sooner
this way to show off true
than bend that way like men
likewise to you--
        they try . . .
and there turns my head,
                too--
this cureless weathercock!

If suff'ring things conjunctively
means less of me, more shining you
should burn like sun
(whom I do brave while you fair block)
you *could* ask me
        (of skin not feared)
to ply the screen directly to my heart,
which lonely lunged unribbed
and sucked for life your airs,
but fool-proof cast now takes,
blood rarefied, looks ducked,
eyes squinting even'n shade--
submitting bidden black

to do their pupils' trade.

If only good
first light could clear
my head looked up
and satisfied--

horizon lush on fire to burning heights
would staff gypped hands with *here I am*!—
no pitied anxious down-turned swipes

where you've tumbled
men to stand 'em,
where men tender
women 'till churned.

My darling, muse-like still
you word me, thing-quipped,
to open red
pledged avid lips
that press and part
to plumb pat dumb
partaken *yes*--
guest lapping comes
eclipsing doom
as pent pleas singe
and suture wounds--

    amor fati!

Blood errs feet first.

Throat thirstily
rings mount-gut moisture
past mooning teeth.
Verse bilks clods cured.
Long-handled tongues
spoon owed seas, lured
to wicked depths.

Louis Petrich is a Tutor at St. John's College in Annapolis, MD.

Dakota Poe

Blurred Lines

Fingers extended, I wave my palm through thick cosmic brush
Thorns & Nebulas
Tree Bark & Comets
Chokecherries & Stars
A final moon landing, dreamer's weave to your fingertips

I watch you light a cigarette, one corner of your mouth turned down
into a paradoxical arc
Fumble with the pack, torn on one side, fading yellow, tucked into
your shirt pocket
Lucky Strike-
Is it lucky enough? You laugh at the absurdity of it all
    and the moonlight dances off your brow. Tiny shadows of super-
novae remnants.
Man in the Moon across your cheek
I've heard he plays a mean guitar...

Clay drips off my wrists, cold, like celestial snow;
    I try to find the texture to mold your permanence.

The Prodigal Phoenix, born on Mars
    from ashes of pasts unrequited and a present unfulfilled
Little fire baby, I swaddle your flames, but they only grow bigger.
We grow scared of the warmth... seek comfort in it too.
Extinguishable Existentialism.

Our burnt tongues find a passionate release in holding hands...

You lay on my couch and ask "What's the point of it all?"
Green eyes round, large, and eager to witness this final destination of
our intertwined stories
I tell you I don't know, but I wish I did.

A tear swims its way down my chin, pooling at the neck where my
heartbeat can be heard
                    singing in tune to the riffs of your guitar.
We choke, cry, laugh, breathe.
You touch my cheek, and I am back home.
Ascend into brilliancy of a cloudless sky.

Destined for madness, our eyes brim with the pleasure of this chaotic
beauty-
never truly separated from
the quiet longing, for you, my love.

Dakota Poe graduated from Washington College on the Eastern Shore
of Maryland with a degree in International Studies and a concentra-
tion in Women's Studies. Writing poetry, traveling, cinema, and ask-
ing useless hypothetical questions are amongst her most passionate
pastimes; she is proud to be able to say she shares a direct lineage
with the master of mystery and macabre himself, Edgar Allan Poe.

Matthew Powell

Monster

some say that love heals
not me
I wish I couldn't feel
I gave someone
what was left of me

she is a monster in the shadows
deep within my heart
which has been drained of blood
cold and blue

she is the darkness in my soul
the poison in my veins
nightmares
burned into my brain

you are so beautiful
you turn my dark
cold nights
into the brightest
summer days
chasing this monster away

love
is the harbinger of pain

I adore you
I wish you would stay
so I need you
to go away

Matt has been writing poetry since his early teen years as a form of therapy. He typically writes bout his experiences with heartbreak and death, but he has also ventured into world history and current political events. He has been heavily influenced by music and other poets such as: Taylor Swift, The Birthday Massacre, Rise Against, Edgar Allan Poe, Sylvia Plath, and Lang Laev. He is working on his own book of poetry which will be entitled "Barbed Wire" and released in early 2023. He currently lives on Maryland's eastern shore with beloved miniature pinschers Lucy and Ozzy.

Anne Andrews Province

Fresh Fallen Snow

Snow globe
you shake me up with your swirling snow
like shattered ice broken
my childhood spills open
a snow burst of memories spills in
of warm toasty mittens
snowmen and sleigh rides
snow angel silhouettes
siblings by my side
too cold to stay outside
but never wanting to come inside
until your hot cocoa kiss
and though I was born of summer
I was snuggled in your womb
in the blizzard of 66
My Dad caught the last flight to Guam
while Mother Earth drifted against our door
you Mothered us four
Crystal ball now I know
you were the peace and beauty
of fresh fallen snow.

Anne A. Province has lived in Maryland her entire life (and that's a long time!). She has lived on a sailboat, traveled the Chesapeake and ICW waterways to the Bahamas, hiked the Grand Canyon, worked with alligators, large snakes arachnids, hedgehogs and more. She is passionate about writing poetry, traveling, hiking and LOVING all animals!.

Michael Puglia

Impossible?

Impossible
That's where i have landed
Same stuff different year
I know what i know
And you may think i am a fool
But i am far from the pool
My knowledge has lead me into a dangerous place more than once
My fluid motion is only in my mind
Yet i am compelled by the beat of the rock
Getting deeper and darker to the truth
Reality warps us all as entropy wins again
The others around you become the focus
And you are never alone, though it always seems
Memories of friend and family outshine the reality of the now
In a silent non verbal place, but easily moved by a communication
not understood by most
Or is it staring into the great unknown which i seem to be familiar
with
And maybe that is why it's not art work on the wall of my grave un-
til i am dead
The wind pushing the tumbleweed, or the ghost ship lost in the tide
I did find her, and had them, and became older me
You don't really get it unless you can really understand and see
How easy it is to sound like Twain, out of context and out of time
Most seem to get you attention with just pushing the profane

But what is art and how does that mix with fame
And if you haven't figured that out, there is no one to blame
Jesus had follower, we are suppose to lead on our own
Coveting others to false affiliations leads us nowhere
Collaboration, imagination, and keeping positive drive real innovation
No time for losers, that does mean time runs out for winners
And who really accounts and measures the how good or young, and the elapsed time of death
And how much media content have you left behind and how long will it be in fashion
When the opposite of sharing equally together is a mistaken dictator
Crashing religions mis matched as their leaders
still control economic and political power bases
As our products cross into our magic items, tri quarters, and belief systems
To form and shape reality for ourselves
Seems impossible

Michael Puglia creator, actor, writer, teacher. Recently he's been shopping on a fantasy novel to publishers and creating and writing for role playing games. He has written poetry most of his life starting in earnest at the age of thirteen. He just recently finished his first "monster" supplement for a very popular role playing game. He is married and they have two children and enjoy traveling together and going on adventures as a family.

J.M. Recchia

Kismet

Like title sequences…
wrinkled reruns scrolled charily
from the backs of my lids.
A closed airing.

Days when time didn't exist.
And streets were playgrounds.
And cloud shuttles departed daily to undiscovered worlds.
When the moon was still made of cheese.
And we thought we could fly.
When the magical realm of Fae still held sway.
When rain didn't need umbrellas.
That peculiar first kiss.

....

With just a scrap of me left…
and the kismet immortal,
I return home unpeopled.

Hearing nothing more than
the welcomed, cushy sound
of the furnace firing off
its summer heat…
hissing in drudgery…

and the days freshly fallen snow
still clinging to my clothes.

J.M. Recchia is a striving, not to be confused with starving writer. Although the latter would no doubt be the case, if not for the present means by which he procures the necessary provisions for his continued existence. He's a creative director for his own ad agency in Baltimore, MD. He's had numerous short stories and poems published by the Maryland Writers Association, the Maryland Bard Association and The Washington Writers Publishing House. "Bones," a short story was also selected for first place, for a winter themed short story, by the Maryland Writers Association.

Vina Hutchinson Roberts

Streets and Seasons

These streets, as he mocks them,
surround me for reasons.
These streets protect me
From a thousand harms.
I have loved but not him
and love is like seasons.
They come and they flee
while I hide from his charms.

Vina Hutchinson Roberts is an award-winning writer, editor, and historian with BA degrees in journalism and history and an MA in American history. In 2018, she was diagnosed with Stage 3 cancer. Now thankfully in remission, she is using her life in survivorship to accomplish lifelong hopes and deferred dreams, taking her newfound confidence in herself to achieve her goals and serve as a role model for positivity and survivorship.

Carolyn L. Robinson

Dream

I dreamed about you again,
but this time you were a cloud.
I admired you for hours
fixed so solidly in the clear blue sky.
You looked like a cotton ball
at first and I thought of all
the ways I'd hold you.
Between my fingers -
Stuffed into my ear -
Wrapped in plastic between my legs.

I thought if I spun you
and turned you into thread
that I could wear you draped around my shoulders,
tucked into my jeans,
and you would be my favorite t-shirt.

But, I didn't want to change you -
realized you were already so right.
So there I stood,
feet glued to the ground -
eyes fixed on your perfectly irregular form
against a perfect blue sky

and I realized
it didn't matter what package you came in -
I'd love you anyway.

Carolyn L. Robinson has published eight poetry books to date in addition to writing children's stories and activity books and has had her poetry published in several anthologies as well. She is committed to keeping the arts alive in the communities around Baltimore. She is the curator of a bi-weekly open mic in Baltimore called CJ's Place. She enjoys traveling and all things creative. You may contact her on IG @LovePoet18 or @CJsPlace_18.

Shubhrangshu Roy

the honeysuckle

This Universe, and everything we see of it,
Is make-belief.
You make.
I believe.
You unmake.
I remake.
Come to think of it:
Your dream. My daydream.
Your darkness. My delusion.
Someone's already been there, done that!
It's just that the patterns keep changing
While I peep inside your kaleidoscope.
So, be warned. I am not the eternal, ephemeral virgin.
Your mind is just another honeysuckle that blooms
In sunshine.
There's no point running between fact and fiction.
It's the chase alone that jostles for space.
Then what's the truth really about?
Does it exist?
You need to dig deeper. And deeper.
Now, and forever.
For, you can never immerse in the nectar of the honeysuckle
That dips its head in shame.
Small wonder, then, the dip is so frightfully deep.
Do I need to dive the depths to suckle … the honey?

I must find out.

Which is why you must ask.

Or is it that you are timid? Too scared.

Did I ever try, and choke on breath?

Did I ever dive and drown?

Because you were so much in love with your pleasing crimson petals.

And that's alright.

Because that illusory ideal may well lead the honeysuckle

To its best flush yet.

Sometimes, your lie can lead me to my own truth: I can.

After all, it's all mental contortion.

Like the butterfly curling its snoot on itself.

For, once the monarch butterfly uncurls its snoot to suckle the honey,

It invariably curls it back again to the vast emptiness where it belongs,

Each curl a subtle interruption in the flow

Of the nectar that oozes forth from within you, the honeysuckle.

Each flutter of the wings, a chant that strings together this Universe.

Come to think of it. Think hard.

Shubhrangshu Roy is a Bethesda-based poet and storyteller. His two works, published by Hay House, are Shadows of the Fragmented Moon (May 2022), a composition of 108 mystic chants, and Zara's Witness (March 2019), a work of mythical literature. Roy is currently working on decoding the secrets of Hinduism.

Eric Ruark

In Search of Lost Time

From the gray ruins of my memory
She rises like a shadow vague and unsteady
Shrouded in deep gloom,
Only to ignite in preternatural light
Rekindling the images of a lost time.

The beauty of the woman framed amid
Golden curls loose to the evening breeze,
Her large lustrous eyes pinion my soul.
I offer her my heart and suffer the agonies
Of what might have been.

Rejecting my heart, I took hers
Capturing her unparalleled beauty
In the abstraction of a decaying
Object I could hold in my hands.

She floats away in an unreal dance
A dream too bright to last
Death keeps an open house.
We will meet again.

Eric Ruark's short stories have appeared in the United State in Alfred Hitchcock's Myster Magazine and in Canada in Mystery Weekly. In addition to loving mystery stories, he also has a penchant for the Gothic as inspired by Edgar Allen Poe.

Edward Lewis Scheiderer

Premonition

There is within me premonition
An only half-lit precognition
Existing only dimly seen
And yet I sense profoundly keen
Upon the edges of my mind
A path which soon will be designed

Elusive vision yet to be
Affecting my reality
The vague appearing certainty
Of some eventuality
While coming near -
Remains unclear

Is my fate an open book
Into which I briefly look,
With pages writ by unseen hand,
Upon hard stone - or shifting sand?
Should I take this premonition,
As a sign of that condition,
Of a future inching slow,
chiseled with a hammer's blow?

With the destined path ahead
Onto which I will be led,

Grooved in granite, all ordained
By fate my movement hard restrained?

Or is this obscure premonition
Open to my own volition,
A path resembling pouring grains
contoured much like the hour-glass drains?

With what paths may lie ahead
Onto which I could be led,
I know not where my answers lie,
And if the fates all choice deny,

But book now writ,
With path full-lit,
Premonition close attend,
I turn the page;
walk 'round the bend.

Winner of Baltimore County's 2018 Silver Pen Writing Contest for poetry, Edward Lewis Scheiderer is a retired 78 year-old, who walked a Postman's route for decades while composing stories and poems. His wife dubbed him a "man of letters!" He grew up from the Atlantic to the Pacific as a Coast Guard brat; graduated from the University of Maryland; was a Vietnam veteran of the "Tonkin Gulf Yacht Club" and settled in Maryland.

James I Schempp

Bright September Sky

Driving the Celica, top down
Long Island Expressway,
Heat shimmering off the pavement
Radio blaring to overcome
The wind in my Oticons.
The morning is warm and sultry
And the wind is tussling my hair
In those moments when the traffic
Allows me to move the gear-shift
Out of second.
I adjust my Ray Bans
Because of the reflection in the window
Of an SUV that just cut in
And made me brake,
Hoping this will be the worst thing
I'll have to deal with today.
On NPR they're talking about
Some random airplane,
Maybe a private plane,
Maybe a military,
Off course,
Flying over Manhattan.
No one knows.

James I Schempp was born and raised on the high plains of the Midwest, just outside Bismarck. His journey has so far led him to the west in Colorado, to the East in New York and now to the Mid-Atlantic in Maryland. An actor and designer by training and a playwright and poet by avocation he knows that language and communication is the basis of humanity.

Ginda Simpson

The Caregiver

Do not judge me
unless you have walked in my shoes.
The Caregivers' Road is roughly paved,
cracked and riddled with potholes
and enough debris
to have worn out my shoes long ago.
I have been forced to walk
barefoot.

Not an invitation to stroll
across the green velvet softness
of a grassy meadow at dawn
Nor
along the cool gritty moisture
of a sandy beach at sunset

No,
while caring for the man I love
who suffers the devastation
of a disease with no cure
I walk
barefoot
Across fields of broken glass
and streets of burning coals.

On my shoulders
I carry a rod with the weight of steel
on each end is a frayed basket
which I try to balance
his needs, my needs,
many of which fall through the cracks.

I have been known
to have sudden outbursts,
punctuated by bad, bad language
tasteless, graceless
emotional earthquakes
coming from a place of
unspeakable anguish.

Please, I beg you,
do not judge me.

Ginda Simpson is a painter and a poet. Her published works include several memoirs and monthly travel stories for a British magazine in Egypt. She is married, mother to three daughters, and grandmother to five. Now a resident of Easton, Maryland, Ginda was born in Baltimore, but has lived in Germany, Italy, and Egypt.

Kate M. Sine

Daisy

passes the cigarette down the next link in the chain
sending the torch with a fuchsia lip stain soldered at the filter,
an imprint of the memory of when she first inhaled,
felt him press against her lungs like flowers,

fresh

cut
flowers.

Kate M. Sine graduated from Frostburg State University in December 2017. They serve the community as a Public Service Librarian at the local library. They have a poem entitled "Coffee" in the College of Southern Maryland's Spring 2020 edition of their literary magazine, *Connections,* as well as the poem "Old Bay," published in the 2020 edition of *Maryland Bards Poetry Review.*

Elizabeth Singletary

His Love Her Heart

She
lived
and breathed
his embrace
with ardent fondness
Moments to cherish forever
Intimately shared hours of laughter and silence
Loving, not always agreeing
Forever adored
Tenderness
covered
her
heart

Elizabeth relocated to Capitol Heights, MD (Prince George's County) for a short period before moving to Washington, DC and continues to work in Prince George's County, MD. She won honorable mention for a poetry submission to Bethesda Urban Partnership, her essay "Value in Brokenness" appeared in "Awake Our Hearts" online newsletter, and she was featured in James P. Wagner's (Ishwa) guide and workbook on Grid Poems. She has participated in several Local Gems Chapbook Challenges where she has broadened her scope, discipline, and joy of poetry writing. Elizabeth writes for inspiration, healing, and hope.

Alex Smith

Bay Hundred Ghost Dance

Old graves in a fresh corn field,
A wooden crab basket nestled in a rubber inner tube,
Floating lazily on the Chesapeake,
A cigarette pack rolled up in a t-shirt sleeve,
Ready to scoop up the beautiful swimmers,
Not far from where Frederick Douglass had his reckoning,
Not far from where Dorothy Lamour danced on wooden floors,
Not far from where Barry Goldwater sat cussing in a phone booth,
Swearing at the same God as young Fred Douglass,
Forever dreaming of Dorothy Lamour,
Lives intermingled that never touch,
Old souls in a pitch-black fever dream,
A ghost dance for the ages on the Bay Hundred shores.

Alex Smith is a poet and writer living in the historic village of Sherwood on Maryland's Eastern Shore. A former award-winning journalist and marketing executive, Alex owns a boutique business advisory firm - Kairos LLC - and coaches and mentors aspiring business leaders. His passions include travel, music, pickleball, and boating on the Chesapeake Bay and Talbot County's amazing creeks and rivers.

Patrice Smith

Common Ground

A sacred place where like minds meet
and hopeful hearts converge at the intersection
of some obscure unspoken thought
while positioned in the middle of a busy familiar avenue
where fleeting friendships often leave their faded
watermarks on the corners of unfulfilled desires

Patrice Smith, is a life-long resident of the Washington DC area and long term educator. She is a keen observer of the human condition and expresses her thoughts about these sensory impressions through poetry and spoken word. Patrice aspires to touch the mind, heart, and soul through her writings.

Mary Ellen South

Winter Provides

Winter provides a time to rest
To take stock of our lives
To slow down and value what we have
To know who we are.

Winter provides a time to dream
Of times we had long ago
Long days and long nights
Where reflection takes priority.

Winter provides a time to care
The giving season comes alive
 Gratitude for family and friends
Faith recognized as a priority.

Winter provides a time to know
 That even though it's dreary and cold
A promise of spring is soon to come
We need this respite to gather who we are.

Mary Ellen is a retired educator with a entrepreneurial career as well. She has been writing poetry for over sixty years when as a young widow she found respite in sharing her sorrow through the written word. Her works have been published in many various media. She is a member of the Rehoboth Beach Writers Guild but now resides in Maryland where she was born and raised.

Tom Squitieri

Out The Window

Can I just be one of you
I don't care how long
Please, just let me

There must be a reason
So many of you came to me
To the window
Beyond knowing I needed you
with smiles
calls
Touching through the pane
Pollinating peace, beauty,
To my soul
Restoring invulnerability of
Forever away dreams to my mind
Your beams, waiting to transport me
Drawn into the sky with morning tableaus
The spirit opens

I know your lives are brief
then you are gone
I am already gone here
So let me flutter with you
To bring magic and joy
And see the world in beauty

Tom Squitieri is a three-time winner of the Overseas Press Club and White House Correspondents' Association awards for work as a war correspondent. His poetry appears in several publications and venues. He writes most of his poetry while parallel parking or walking his dogs, Topsie and Batman.

Dave Stant

Final Goodbye

Moonlight shines through a halo in the clouds
Dim light illuminates her deep brown eyes
Snow falls quietly on the campus grounds
I'm saddened to think how time passed by
You gazed softly into eyes filled with tears
A star crossed love in truth never prevails
A memory of goodbye reappears
Into the snow white night my ship sets sail
You touched me gently with your soothing touch
A captive of your beauty now set free
Years later thoughts of you became too much
I never grasped how much you meant to me
A moonless eve completes this brief romance
If only to have this eternal dance

David Stant remembers watching the snow fall from his apartment window at Frostburg State University. His mind wanders to his time at the University of Maryland and his first love interest while there. In the present tense, he remembers her touching him on the cheek and looking into his eyes knowing this would be the last time he'd see her. He hopes to one day see her again.

Jordan Stewart

Eraser

Prose written along my person,
you're graphite smudged across my tongue.
No space for anything else
on this canvas,

what else is there to do but destroy?
You make room for your imprint,
such an imperfect mark on the
parts of myself I never loved before.

Now that you're gone
there's nothing
but blank space and the
echo of what was.
I'm left wishing I could erase her

but this eraser doesn't take away,
it only spreads black across white
pages and now everything is dark.

You were a work of art, and
I wanted more than just to stare
from across the room.
I wanted what I could feel,
something I could touch,

taste, smell.

I remind myself that great works
of art are built upon.
So I hang myself to dry,
waiting for the next
person to come round and
paint over what once was.

Your signature remains
on the bottom of my heart,

I hope I left a mark on you too.

Jordan is a black, non-binary queer poet from Baltimore, MD. He gathers inspiration from every part of life to create his art. With his work he mainly hopes to foster a deep sense of connection and emotion between reader, writer, and the world we live in.

Jeff Swiss

Why Artists Always Seem To Wear Black

or

Loads of Fun*

Loads of fun… this creative energetic atmosphere
and actual name of the building, this…
'in the moment experience', where we find ourselves with our
friend Edna.
delight, I didn't even care about the black smear
on my favorite cream colored pants by
brushing up against a dirty sill climbing
out the window of Edna and David's art studio.
We did this to go up the fire escape to the roof to
take in this vibrant, creative city on a beautiful spring day.

Being above offers quite a view of a festival happening
down below across the street... a rock band plays in a MICA**
open parking lot. A young woman sings in a lush syrupy
flowing voice. Two guitarists weaving a slow, dreamy
slightly bluesy counterpoint, playing in sync with
the bass player's open notes woven with the soft spacious
rhythm of the drummer. The listener pleasantly greeted
with layers of infused sound that's deep, whole, rich, warm…
inviting to the ear and soul on a perfect Saturday afternoon…

163

As the music rises, it reverberates off the walls all around the buildings, thrumming thru
the streets. A large banner spread across the fence catches my eye
with these four words...

'The universe doesn't work.'

So I can't help thinking if the person expressing this sentiment got
a stain on their favorite pants
or shirt, maybe their jacket, you know... the one just worn on
special occasions. It could be they
have not had the chances to get what they really wanted from or
out of life or they got what
they thought they wanted, were mistaken and have to deal
with the consequences.

But for the three of us up on the roof, taking it all in... the universe,
for now at least seems to
be working just fine even with the black smudge on
my favorite cream pants...

it's still loads of fun...

And on the way home you turn toward me, smile and say
"no wonder artists always seem to wear black"

* 'Loads of Fun', is an artist's studio co-op now called 'The Motor House', In The North Avenue Arts District,
    right on North Avenue in Baltimore.

** Maryland Institute College of Art

Jeff Swiss is a proud Baltimorean born and raised and still lives in the city. His high school English teacher, Russ Connelly, inspired and encouraged him to write, which he still does. Jeff is also a songwriter.

Amanda Taylor

How I Got to You

I had to kiss a hundred frogs.
Swim through a river of tears.
Wish upon a million stars.
Pray you'd come my way until I had bruises on my knees.
Break a dozen hearts.
Have my heart broken three times as much.
Go on a journey of self-discovery.
Wallow in self-pity.
Fight to return to normalcy.
Discover my purpose.
Find my place in the world.
Kiss more frogs.
Overcome another existential crisis.
Realize the beauty within me.
And fall deeply in love with myself.
Appreciate the benefits of being single.
Learn how to pursue my bliss.
God took me through the ringer, so I'd be prepared for a time like this.
The moment when I looked into your beautiful eyes and realized this is it.

Amanda Taylor is a nonprofit professional and lifelong Maryland resident. She earned an undergraduate degree from Bowie State University and later earned two graduate degrees from University of Maryland Global Campus (formerly University of Maryland University College). Amanda has a deep appreciation for artistic endeavors and shares her creations with the world under the moniker AunTay. Her poems **To the Rose Amongst the Weeds** and **I Wish** were selected for the 2020 and 2022 Maryland Bards Poetry Review.

Brenardo Taylor

Memory Box...An Ode To Christmas

3 pm
Settling in
Celebrating Holidays with Family and Friends
I open up a music box and watch the ponies spin
And it begins

I see the bright of Christmas lights, sparkling, shining, blinking
I hear the mounds of angels sounding joy in how they're singing
I hear the tales of Christmas bells of proclamations ringing
I am shrinking under covers to remember Christmas past
Lovers, mothers, fathers, brothers, sisters, and their laughs
In spirits that are frayed these days, this is what I grasp
To bring the smile
To hold awhile

I think of table settings with food in such abundance
Candles, bowls, and ribbons look so mystical and wondrous
Tears barely being contained sometimes when I think upon this
I am wishing for return to days when this is what I knew
I marvel at those years gone by and how those memories grew
And though they are no longer here, I know that they were true
Love and smiles
That stayed awhile

I see my parents struggle to be stern with so much mirth

I hear songs calling fervently that there be peace on earth
Other songs are focused on the meaning of a birth for a child
Of Love and smiles
To hold a while
And now they pile
Back into the memory box of mine

Brenardo is a Poet and Songwriter who has resided in Maryland since 1969. He has been writing poetry for over 50 years and presented poetry all around the world. In 2020 Brenardo was cited as a Poet Of Excellence for Prince George's County.

Kelly Michelle Thomas

Conversation of Trees

Have you heard it?
The conversation among the trees?
Filled with a language only known by the leaves
Of rustles and whispers carried by the westward wind
Bellowing through the statures so proper and prim
Gliding along the branches that dance and bend
As if they are filled with laughter among family and friend

Listen darling, hear the cheers
Close your eyes, let the woodland whisper to your ears
Hear the woodpecker ah' peckering, while the katydids cry
The crows ah' crowing, while the squirrels scurry and climb
From limb to limb, can you hear the timbers split?
As if they are sharing secrets full of chatter and gossip

Can you hear it?

The rustles...

  The whispers...

    The creatures...

      The splitting timbers...

Carried by the westward wind
Bellowing through the statures so proper and prim
Gliding along the branches that dance and bend

Are laughters among family and friend
Sharing secrets full of chatter and gossip

This is the conversation of trees

Kelly Michelle Thomas is a visual artist and poet born on March 25, 1989 in Silver Spring, MD where she attended James Hubert Blake High School. Kelly is the author of the poetry series, *125 Days,* self-published in 2021 and 2022.

Rochelle Thompson

It's the weekend (Now that's what's up!)

Weekends are a time of relaxation
When you are worn out, you need some rejuvenation
So whatcha gonna do with yours?

Are you going to the mall and stepping into all the stores
Or are you gonna shoot hoops with your boys until the sweat falls
from your pores
Are you gonna laugh with your friends and have some fun
Or will you be stuck in your room till your chores or homework gets
done
Will you do something as a volunteer?
Or will you be off at a game struttin' a new cheer

Will little brothers and sisters, as usual, be all up in your grill
Or will your parents take them out so you can just chill

Will you call to thank your grandma who bought you that hot new
phone?
Or will you be ungrateful and instead text your friends some suspect
messages,
acting like you grown!

Will you gather together and confess who makes you giggle
Or will you chat on Snapchat about a relationship that fizzled?

Get it all out or get it all in, for that's what the weekend is all about
For the weekend soon will come to an end my friend

Did you pause to thank the Creator?
When it's Sunday afternoon do you still have plans for later?
With Sunday night, the weekend is over and we all know that on Monday you'll hate to roll over.
Well, no need to frown, no need to let it get you down
You need some rest, so you'll be at your best
Ready to face the week's challenges and plan some more for another cool weekend
that begins on Friday at 2:25pm when you step out the school door.

Weekends are a time of relaxation.
When you are worn out, you need rejuvenation
So whatcha gonna do with yours?

Rochelle Thompson, a New Jersey native recently retired from the Prince George's County school district in Maryland. During her tenure as a School Librarian she enjoyed sharing her original poems and stories with students and faculty alike. She began writing poetry in high school and now delights in sharing her "You did it again" President Obama poem. Her family treasures her poetry written for birthdays, homegoing celebrations, retirements and weddings. All look forward to her future writings as well.

Ruth Ticktin

Upwards Look

Sunlit skies
dreamy days
The one and always

Sing and dance
speak and draw
the miraculous
Lifting in motion

Sun climbs over cloud wisps
murky waters wave on

Give seeds of solace
add in drops of joy
Raise up eyes and voice

With rites or not lay down
soak up what is offered

Too hot too cold look
upwards on high choose
chances to rejoice

Ruth Ticktin has coordinated programs, advised, and taught English in DC and MD since 1977. Encouraging shared stories, she is Author: Was Am Going, Recollections Poetry & Flash (NewBayBooks 2022.) Co-author: Psalms (PoeticaPublish 2020.) What's Ahead? (ProLinguaLearning 2013.) Contributor: BendingGenres (2018-19); Art in Covid-19 (SanFedelePress.)

Alan Vandervoort

Mohican River

Chose to paddle upstream
To see what others pass by
Floating reserved for another day
Another experience

Muscles challenge the flow
Creating waves against the canoe
Sunrays flash in and out of sycamore leaves
And attack dragonfly wings

A majestic great blue launches from the shallows
The rattle of a kingfisher heard overhead
Catch a glimpse of a sneaky green heron
And indulge in the art of counting rope swings

The sun will be low and shoulders sore
When the day's destination is reached
A small twig fire provides companionship
Stars say well done, deserved rest

Alan Vandervoort of Baltimore, Maryland, is a novelist and poet. In his free time, he works on short stories, screenplays, articles, and book reviews. His debut novel is *Sandhills – A Novel* with a second novel, *Key Largo Summer,* published in 2019. Alan describes his writings as explorations of human emotions in association with a variety of relatable enthusiasms.

Joseph Vivens

Where did Judas go?

Where did Judas go?
the base of our plates
start to grow cold
we wait to say grace
sunset bells toll
Where did Judas Go?
The smell of fresh bread
start to grow stale
our wine is still red
the yeast's now ale
Where did Judas Go?
The chalice's lip
Ruby as loves kiss
As we all take sips
The Father asks this

Joseph Vivens is the author/creator of the Chunky And Friends children's book series. He is an English major with a concentration on Creative Writing at Bowie State University and lives in Rockville, MD with his wife and two kids.

Kaitlin Wachter

Pandora's Box

It's a treasure chest, of darkest wood
carved, solid and banded
By a set of ornate iron hasps
Its hardwood smoothly sanded

The key in its old-fashioned lock
Is heavy and gilt-plated
And seals the fabric memories
A lifetime, neatly folded

Textiles collected over my years
Some bold and some faded
But each an aspect of myself
Unique -- valued, or hated

Sometimes I pull out favorite things
None alike and technicolor
Strutting 'round to flaunt my weird
Bold and feminine fluttered

But only when there's no one home
To view my act transgressed
For propriety must be maintained
Portions of me suppressed

Most times the lid is shut and locked
The contents still within
None of them abolished by the wood
But muffled from their din

A voice of truth whispers low
I should be unashamed
The fabric of my life is me
Despite others' blame

Yet the catch holds tight against them
Despite the inner critic
It allows none to leave or enter
Lest Pandora's mimicked

To keep temptation well at bay
The key is confiscated
By persons loved, of good intent
But unwittingly thwarted

But once I regain the taken key
Unlock the iron clasp
The crazy colors liberated
And I'm myself at last

Kaitlin Wachter has been writing poetry since childhood. She loves
to experiment with wordplay, styles, and rhythms. Her biggest inspi-
ration comes from everyday beauty and experiences.

Anne King Whaples

When Elephants Die

Behemoths draped in mourning gray,
gently touch the bones of another;
sit shiva for days.
Tentative touch of trunk,
a gentle finger, finds
reassurance along the jaw,
teeth, tusks. This search for the familiar
continues in silence so deep birds don't sing.
A slow blowing of air
resonates in an African wilderness
where one who died alone is buried by many.
Leaves and twigs rain down
to cover dusky skin in a final act of dignity.
Are they truly grieving?
Can we ever know?
Silence, ritual, distress.
Touch, bones, dust.

Loss.

Anne King Whaples has been writing poetry since high school. She majored in journalism at The Ohio University and spent her career writing for newspapers and managing non-profit communications. She studied with poet Michael Waters while working on her Masters at Salisbury University. Now retired, still writing poetry, Anne lives in Cambridge, Maryland.

Aressa V. Williams

Told Your Mother

At a neighborhood friend's cookout
Forty years after we broke-up,
Your mother grabbed my hands, looked in my eyes,
asked me.
"What happened? You were supposed to be my daughter-in law."
I smiled, pleased that she felt that way about me.
My honest answer surprised both of us.
                    Told your mother.
"Too young, immature, selfish, the marriage would not have
worked."
Your mother responded,
"I married Anthony's father when I was eighteen. We worked."
She spoke as if you and I could have done the same.
Told your mother.
"I would not have made your son a good wife."
"Spoiled, bossy while you never complained."
"Fussy for no reason, but you forgave my poor behavior."
"I want to be a virgin when we get married." My selfish mantra.
Respectful, patient you agreed. No pressure.
Family assumed we would wed after high school.
You joined the Air Force; I went to college.
My "Dear John" letter broke your heart.
Told your mother.

Breaking up with you taught me lessons.
Never write hurtful letters.
Never take extraordinary kindness for granted.
Never throw away a priceless mink coat for a cheap denim jacket.

Aressa V. Williams, retired English Professor, is an active member of Pen in Hand, Poetry X Hunger, Poetry Nation. The word weaver, a Prince Georges County Literary Leader and the Write Women's poet laureate, is currently writing her memoir. She calls her poems "word-snapshots" that invite readers to imagine.

Ed Williams

Threescore Years Or More?

Set your wisdom deeply in our hearts
finished with nothing but a sigh
like a night's sleep soon forgotten

Replace our years of trouble with decades of delight
finished with nothing but a sigh
like glistening grass that springs up one day

Replace our years of trouble with decades of delight
dry and withered the next
like glistening grass that springs up one day
you will give us success in all we do
dry and withered the next
let your sweet beauty rest upon us
you will give us success in all we do

Set your wisdom deeply in our hearts
let your sweet beauty rest upon us
like a night's sleep soon forgotten

---

ed williams, jr is an ELA teacher in St. Mary's County who enjoys writing pantoums, a style he discovered in college in a creative writing class.

Melisa Wilmot

One Day

One day,
I'll find the words
I meant to say
and I will say them
with conviction

One day,
words will fly
from me and
I will capture them
in stories of my own

One day,
you'll just be a memory
recorded into a journal
and I will forget you
were ever there

One day,
I'll write a happy ending
and you'll know it's your fault
that I couldn't ever find
those happy words before

Melisa Wilmot holds a master's degree in Teaching Writing from Johns Hopkins University and a bachelor's degree in English Literature from the University of South Florida St Petersburg. She has been a professor, teacher, advisor, and retail specialist. She lives at home with her family and their feisty French Bulldog, Maggie. Melisa dedicates her work in honor of her mom, who always taught her to strive to do better, and Melville, for his unconditional love.

William Heath Wroten

The way you mourn....

You think it's about you, but the time will soon tell.

Blanketed bustles, as you cover your head, to not wake up the world with your tears.

The grass has died, where your things have sat, staunch, unmoved, in ...my yard.

Sunrise to set, those reminders, fossils they've become , of this decade onced lived.

Your ego sees obsession, reality is the life you promised, you can never deliver.

Go away peasant, go into the night, I've been crowned the king of this life I lead now.

Lady Madonna, ...or Medusa, tattle tale of hearts , you are gone.
Give back my time, you shall have your dignity. Go..

Born and raised on the eastern shore of Maryland, William Heath Wroten, 46 years young, small business owner, made the jump to poetry, after 41 years of playing music. It goes hand in hand, poems , songs for the eyes.

Mengtong Xiang

13 Minutes

13 minutes of deafening words,
And I was left no choice but to stay here forevermore.
Past withered wood and clouded window panes, I wallow in my fantasy of
Sleepless nights healed by a single touch,
Mundane days livened by a single call,
Overcast afternoons lightened by a single smile,
And languid mornings brightened by a single kiss.
13 minutes of numbing disbelief,
And I was left no choice but to sit cross-legged in the restaurant forevermore.
"Did you ever hear about the girl who got frozen?" they whisper,
Stealing glances at the peeling, gray wood that made up my eternal
quarters.
13 minutes of deafening, heart-wrenching silence,
And I was left no choice but to sit and stare at his vacated chair forevermore.
I still clutch a wine-stained napkin,
A glass shard,
And his golden chain.
13 minutes of delusion when my fantasy ended,
And I was left no choice but to wait for him to realize he's got it
wrong forevermore.
"I've met someone else," his lips had uttered, and I could no longer
bear witness.

Dust collected on my pinned-up hair,
A mascara-streaked tear wavered in time,
And a pale scar lingered from shattered glass.
13 minutes of my last breaths of sanity,
And I was left no choice but to pine for how it was supposed to be
forevermore.
I refused to share perspectives,
Move on,
Grow older,
And leave the restaurant.
13 minutes and everyone becomes a critic,
Their condescending scowls piercing.
13 minutes and everyone believes they know better,
"Heartbreak happens every day, there's no need to lose it."
13 minutes and I stay young forever,
Lamenting over a 20s break-up.
13 minutes and I haunt the corner in the restaurant,
Hoping that he doesn't have a wife.
13 minutes and I live in a fantasy,
Minding my business with only him on my mind.
13 minutes and I stay here forevermore.

Mengtong Xiang is 14 years old and from Potomac, Maryland. She attends Takoma Park Middle School and enjoys participating in writing competitions. In Mengtong's free time, she frequently reads fantasy novels and crafts her own stories.

Joseph Zuccaro

One Second

I thought I'd see you
When I was walking by,
Thinking I'd play cool
And be cordial at best
I did have every right
To be where I was
As did you that afternoon,
So it would be no surprise

It was a dreary day
And I certainly didn't expect,
If our eyes were to meet,
Sunshine and a rainbow.
And sure enough
Among some familiar faces
Unmistakably clear
Your presence standing out

How could I not look
At someone so paramount
And instrumental
To my new passage
As I waved
Not to get attention
But knowing you'd see me
I had no motive but peace

When our eyes met
I saw a face, neutral
Suddenly drained of joy
Enough to sap mine too.
Suddenly in one second
Somber with reality
Knowing it won't be the same
With no choice but to move on.

Joseph Zuccaro is a professor at Towson University and lives in Baltimore. He is a lifelong resident of Maryland and likes to polka with wildcats. You can find him getting some of his poetry inspiration at the Cat's Eye Pub, Duda's Tavern, or Penny Black in Fell's Point.

Neil Zurowski

I wear them

I wear them
I fold them around me
Tuck them under my banker suit lapels
Wrap myself in them
Tie them tight.

I wear them
All **of** them
Sheer, flocked, lace and brightly hued
Shiny with golden and silver thread
Pima, lambswool and worm spun, Girly
Womanly.

They are not some reckoning with my feminine self
(how could I be gay without you?)
But woven in bergamot, sandalwood, jasmine, and gardenia
They are the hugs
The caressing lips
It is you in the whorls and tassels.

Sadly, Lesser
Every day.

W. Neil Zurowski was born in Washington, D. C. and now resides in Phoenix, MD. A graduate of Gonzaga College High School and The American University, he began writing poetry in the 9th grade inspired by eecummings and supported by Fr. Sampson his English teacher. AMDG,

About the Editor

James P. Wagner (Ishwa) is an editor, publisher, award-winning fiction writer, essayist, historian, performance poet, and alum twice over (BA & MALS) of Dowling College. He is the publisher for Local Gems Poetry Press and the Senior Founder and President of the Bards Initiative. He is also the founder and Grand Laureate of Bards Against Hunger, a series of poetry readings and anthologies dedicated to gathering food for local pantries that operates in over a dozen states. His most recent individual collection of poetry is *Everyday Alchemy*. He was the Long Island, NY National Beat Poet Laureate from 2017-2019. He was the Walt Whitman Bicentennial Convention Chairman and teaches poetry workshops at the Walt Whitman Birthplace State Historic Site. James has edited over 100 poetry anthologies and hosted book launch events up and down the East Coast. He was named the National Beat Poet Laureate of the United States from 2020-2021. He is the owner/operator of The Dog-Eared Bard's Book Shop in East Northport, NY.

Made in the USA
Middletown, DE
16 February 2023

24957072R00113